Inside the Write

Conversations with Ame~~rican~~

Christina Kallas

First published 2014 by
PALGRAVE MACMILLAN

Palgrave Macmillan in the UK is an imprint of Macmillan Publishers Limited, registered in England, company number 785998, of Houndmills, Basingstoke, Hampshire RG21 6XS.

Palgrave Macmillan in the US is a division of St Martin's Press LLC, 175 Fifth Avenue, New York, NY 10010.

Palgrave Macmillan is the global academic imprint of the above companies and has companies and representatives throughout the world.

Palgrave® and Macmillan® are registered trademarks in the United States, the United Kingdom, Europe and other countries.

ISBN 978–1–137–33811–2 hardback
ISBN 978–1–137–33810–5 paperback

This book is printed on paper suitable for recycling and made from fully managed and sustained forest sources. Logging, pulping and manufacturing processes are expected to conform to the environmental regulations of the country of origin.

A catalogue record for this book is available from the British Library.

A catalog record for this book is available from the Library of Congress.

Printed in Great Britain by
CPI Group (UK) Ltd, Croydon, CR0 4YY

To Alex, always

Contents

Acknowledgments

My deep admiration for the work of the dramatic writers presented here and a strong desire to unfold the creative process leading to the work were both the first spark of inspiration and the continuous driving force behind this book. I hope you will enjoy it as much as I have enjoyed having the conversations that make up the biggest part of its contents, and that you will be as fascinated as I was by the recurring themes which I have essayed in my final reflections. Thank you, one and all! Your enthusiasm, and your willingness to respond as openly as possible, made this book. Acknowledgment is also made of the inspiring writers I spoke with at the very early stages, when I was still defining my focus for this book: Peter Blauner, Julie Martin, Howard Korder, thank you! In addition, I would like to thank Baldvin Kári, who was my trusted assistant during the final stages of the book, John Howard and Alison G. Vingiano who read parts of the manuscript and assisted me with their notes, my always supportive agent, Julian Friedmann and, last but not least, Jenna Steventon and Felicity Noble at Palgrave Macmillan: your assistance was a timely and wonderful encouragement. Finally, and with all my love always, to my son Alex: here, a book full of creative, fearless writers – what a beautiful thing!

About the Author

Christina Kallas is a writer-producer for both film and television, professor of film and president of the Federation of Screenwriters in Europe (FSE). Screen credits include the feature films *Mothers* (2010), *The Commissioner* (1998), *I.D.* (1994) and *Liebe Lügen* (1997); several episodes of the Best German TV-awarded series *Edel & Starck* (2002–2005) and *Danni Lowinski* (2010–2012); and the long-form narrative trans-media project *42 Seconds of Happiness* (2011–2014). She is currently teaching at Columbia University's School of the Arts, Film Division, at Barnard College and at the New School for Media Studies in New York City. She earned her BA, MA and PhD in Communication and Media Studies at Freie Universität Berlin, during which time she was a Daimler-Benz-Stiftung fellow. She has previously taught at the German Film and Television Academy Berlin, the International Film School in Cologne and the Film Studies Department of the Aristotle University of Thessaloniki. She is the author of five books in her three writing languages, including *Creative Screenwriting: Understanding Emotional Structure* (London/New York, 2010).

Introduction

High art era

"The popular art of one era is often the high art of the next," wrote the Greek-American literary scholar Alexander Nehamas not so long ago in defense of television, drawing a parallel with Plato's scorn of Ancient Greek drama.[1] TV has long been considered the lesser counterpart to cinema: the place to go in the industry if you couldn't make it into film. For a very long time it was also considered a subject not worthy of academic study. Not so today. With television drama achieving both popular and critical acclaim, it would seem that TV is finally going through its high art era, and that it has emerged from cinema's shadow for good.

Filmmakers have always flirted with television. One has only to recall, from 1980, Rainer Werner Fassbinder's *Berlin Alexanderplatz*, a series of, notably, thirteen 52-minute episodes plus an epilogue, or David Lynch's *Twin Peaks* (1990/1991), which lasted for two seasons, the first with eight and the second with twenty two 50-minute episodes (the pilots were feature-length) or indeed Lars Von Trier's *The Kingdom* (1994), a series of eleven 55-minute episodes. Cinema's flirtation with the new form in fact started much earlier, perhaps with Roberto Rossellini's infamous 1962 news conference where he declared that cinema, the medium for which he had directed such classics as *Rome, Open City* and *Paisan*, was dead and that he would henceforth be making movies for television. Today these filmmakers could be seen as the avant-garde of a form which was still evolving at the time: that of the television series that would educate and elevate rather than just entertain and sell products through advertising. They were interested in reaching the kinds of audience accessible only to broadcasts, but primarily they were fascinated by the possibilities of the long narrative form. "Television allows you to tell a story over time," points out David Lynch, "something cinema doesn't." In the last few years the phenomenon of migration from cinema to TV or from the movie format to the long-form narrative (can *House of Cards*, whose 13 episodes were released on internet platform Netflix in 2013 all on the same day, really be considered television?) has been increasingly gaining momentum, even among established mainstream filmmakers: Steven Spielberg signed the series *The Pacific*, Martin Scorsese *Boardwalk Empire*, and more are sure to follow.

Television's impressive artistic and commercial success is not a solely American phenomenon – it is not even an English-language phenomenon. The case of the Danish series *Borgen* is exemplary. Currently *Borgen* brings together on average a 50% share in its home market and is being shown all over the world to great acclaim. Danish TV drama (featuring shows like *The Killing* and *The Bridge*) began its revival about 15 years ago – at the same time as its domestic film industry, with the fiction department of the public channel DR as its driving force. The positioning of the creator as in American TV series – and the respect for his or her unique "voice" – was reportedly key to that development. Just as American cable TV channels have found success by giving primacy to the writer, DR practices what it calls "one vision."[2]

In this context it is most interesting to observe how things evolved in Europe over time in relation to American TV drama's overwhelming success: for many decades American series were extremely popular in western Europe, so much so that they provoked controversial debates in a number of countries – debates about the dangers of American cultural imperialism and about whether or not state broadcasting systems should be spending public coin to acquire American TV series rather than to produce domestic programs. Then, broadcasters in several European countries started launching their own direct imitations of American TV series. These were not remakes in the classic sense of the word; they were an effort to reproduce the American TV series' success by identifying what worked for them while adapting these elements to the home culture and reality. Eventually, European broadcasters started imitating the American model of the creator-centered show and the writers' room.

This seems to work in certain cases; however, as so often happens with imitation, sometimes it is the less important aspects of the original that are imitated, or the imitator fails to recognize the essence of the original. In fact too little is known about the nuts and bolts of the American model, about its basic working components and the practical aspects of how collaboration works in a writers' room and what the role of the showrunner is in all of its different aspects, as well as his or her relationship with the other writers, with the network and with the studio. In a way this book aims at filling that knowledge gap. If the way American TV drama is created ultimately influences the way quality TV drama is produced elsewhere, at least in the western hemisphere, then it is surely helpful to be able to analyze how and why it is created this way and what the consequences are. This book will take a look beyond what reaches the mainstream media in the frame of a show's promotion and beyond the instructions given in how-to manuals on TV writing. Through a series of conversations with writers from a writer's point of view, the book's goal is to identify what is happening in that writers' room, or in several writers' rooms, and in the writers' minds while they are creating a show – how and what is being written and how it is being produced – and what is the reasoning and the history behind the model we have come to see as responsible for so much creative (and commercial) success.

Three acts of TV history

One could see American TV history as structured in three acts. The first act would comprise the "Golden Age" of the 1950s, with prestigious writers such as Paddy Chayefsky and Rod Serling in the forefront; the second would peak in shows such as *Hill Street Blues* and *Twin Peaks* in the 1980s and 1990s, which laid the groundwork for dramatic complexity through deep characterization and multiple narrative threads found in the US cable series of the last 15 years; which brings us to our third act – series such as *Oz*, *The Sopranos*, *The Wire*, *Boardwalk Empire* and *Mad Men* that have at least two things in common: they are aimed at relatively narrow target audiences[3] and they have developed a highly sophisticated narrative form that seems to borrow from as well as inform cinematic storytelling.

Today, the best American TV drama sweeps away all distinctions between popular and critical success. It becomes the focus of passionate discussion and the locus of narrative experimentation, and has a cultural impact while moving beyond boundaries and challenging the way we think – things which American movies do not seem to do anymore, or to do less and less, writes A.O. Scott.[4] He is not alone in making this comparison. Oscar-winning Italian filmmaker Bernardo Bertolucci has recently[5] referred to the state of the American film industry by saying that "the American films I like now do not come from Hollywood studios but from television series, like *Mad Men*, *Breaking Bad*, *The Americans*" – and he compared these to novels printed in installments in 19th-century newspapers, a comparison we will come to talk about in more detail later. "Apart from a few independent productions," he added, "I think that everything that comes from Hollywood is generally sad. It makes me very sad." Scott explains why: "The traditional relationship between film and television has reversed, as American movies have become conservative and cautious, while scripted series, on both broadcast networks and cable, are often more daring, topical and willing to risk giving offense." The evolution of television drama started in cable with HBO at the forefront (and Showtime, FX or AMC not too far behind) and was then taken up by broadcast network TV. One of the questions which this book will address is why shows of this type were able to develop from these outlets rather than from network TV and what are the main elements which lead to the continuous flow of quality.

One thing can be noted right away: while a lot has been said and written about the moral complexity and sociological density of, say, *The Sopranos* or *The Wire* or indeed *The West Wing*, and about the drive and cultural insight of *Mad Men*, or the spirituality and selection of philosophical topics of *Lost* and the epic dimensions and cinematic production values of *Boardwalk Empire*, the role of the writer as perhaps the most important and influential component of these shows is not stressed enough, or where it is stressed it is discussed in the same manner we discuss the auteur in cinema: as a single genius and not as the representative of a paradigm shift. In comparison with the screenwriter (a term used in the US solely for movie writers) the TV writer has a dissimilarly significant weight. Is the writer's role, which is the one essential difference between the way TV is produced compared to the movies, possibly the main reason for the medium's commercial and artistic success? And if so, how is the writer's role defined in television and what are the main differences from a screenwriter's role in the film industry? There is only one way to find out: talk with the writers – the showrunners and the "number ones" as well as all the other writers at the different levels of the writing staff hierarchy in a writers' room and last but not least the writers-cum-educators who are teaching the upcoming generation of TV writers. After all, what better way to gain real insight into the collaborative process of modern TV writing than by hearing about it from the perspectives of as many writers as possible?

Ultimately, the artistic and commercial success of TV drama is consequential not only for the way we discuss and view TV drama, but also in relation to some of the old unwritten rules, which are currently being rewritten; the crossover of the set boundary between the movies and TV is just one of them. Writers have started to move more freely from one medium to the other. *West Wing* creator Aaron Sorkin, who in 2011 won the Academy Award for *The Social Network*, is perhaps one of the more prominent examples discussed in that context. One will have to wait and see what the effects will be on other traditional practices, concepts and preconceptions that have emerged from cinema, such as the attendant idea that audiovisual storytelling can only result from the mind of a single genius – TV drama actually being the result of collaboration between many writers and minds – or the longstanding practice in the movie industry of the mindless replacing of the original writer or of the writer's exclusion from the set. These concepts and practices in the film industry which potentially put writers at a remove from the end-product are thankfully a world away from the experiences of TV writers – and this may well be an instrumental factor in the artistic and commercial success that we have seen in TV drama.

Long cinematic narrative

Perhaps the biggest challenge to the present status quo and the television–film divide is connected with the oldest question since the birth of the moving pictures: what is cinema? Today, the common consensus is that, with the emergence of new technologies, medium distinctions are becoming increasingly blurred – and we cannot regard any "medium" as an absolute fixed category. Nevertheless, cinema is still considered by many as connected to the darkened theater of the classic period: two uninterrupted hours in the dark; film festivals; theatrical distribution. Many will even indulge in nostalgia and use the term "cinema" only when 35mm film is involved. There is, however, another possible perspective: if we see cinema as storytelling that is (primarily) using image and sound and which is as much about exploration as it is about spectacle, a medium which can penetrate deep into reality by destroying familiar ways of thinking and feeling – by challenging the very frameworks of reality; if we consider Bazin's[6] argument that the idea precedes the invention and hence is superior to the technical means used to achieve it, then it is possible that there is no better term for audiovisual storytelling, none more inclusive, and definitely none which raises the stakes as much as this one does. Eisenstein's vision of cinema as an "excellent instrument of perception"[7] also reminds us how, early on, the function of cinema was debatable, and not taken for granted. Perhaps, once again, we need to stop taking the concept of "cinema" for granted and open the field as generously as we can.

Perhaps cinema is, indeed, everywhere. Perhaps rather than a medium or a concrete format, cinema is a state of mind – and it can be found in TV as well as in the movies.

So should we be discussing some of the TV series considered here as nothing less than long cinematic narratives? And if so, what would that mean?[8] It is fair to say that TV, just half the age of film, has only recently (perhaps in the last 15 years) come into its own. Writers have only recently learned to take advantage of the unique powers of the medium itself. For years the focus was on each episode being a complete story, a standalone. Not only in procedurals but in series generally, the dramatic focus was on the unit of the episode. A TV episode was a mini-movie (much as a web episode is a mini-TV episode now). Then the primary canvas of the TV medium became the season.

According to television lore, the age of multithreading (multiple story threads which would lead through a season or even a whole series) began with the arrival of *Hill Street Blues* in 1981. However, its creator, Steven Bochco, actually applied a technique known and familiar in other genres, that of the soap opera and the sitcom, particularly the half-hour ensemble workplace comedies of the 1970s such as *M*A*S*H*, *The Mary Tyler Moore Show* and *Barney Miller,* which may be considered to be *Hill Street*'s key antecedents. As Steven Johnson says, "Bochco's genius with *Hill Street* was to marry complex narrative structure with complex subject matter,"[9] often confronting difficult social issues while doing so. As Johnson points out, some narratives force you to do work to make sense of them, and part of that cognitive work comes from following multiple threads, keeping often densely interwoven plotlines distinct in your head as you watch. Others even involve the viewer's "filling in": making sense of information that has been either deliberately withheld or deliberately left obscure. A *Hill Street Blues* episode complicated the picture in a number of profound ways. The narrative wove together a collection of distinct strands – sometimes as many as ten, though at least half of the threads involved only a few quick scenes scattered through the episode. There were a large number of primary characters – not just bit parts. And the episode had fuzzy borders, picking up one or two threads from previous episodes at the outset, and leaving one or two threads open at the end.

Before *Hill Street Blues*, the conventional wisdom among television executives was that audiences wouldn't be comfortable following more than three plots in a single episode, and indeed, the first test screening of the *Hill Street Blues* pilot in May 1980 brought complaints from the viewers that the show was too complicated. Today and after decades of experimenting and breaking further boundaries, narrative complexity has reached new, previously inconceivable heights, having come to full bloom in the last ten to 15 years. And although the focus of this book is on American TV drama of that most recent era, it would be unfair to forget that the series we are discussing draw on a long tradition of experimentation with the medium. Ultimately, as Edgerton and Jones point out,[10] a show like, for instance, *The Sopranos* uses strategies perfected over decades and employs "a tradition of visual mastery developed equally in interior spaces and tight, compelling close-ups of soaps, sitcoms, and family melodramas, as well as in the fluid editing and skill at framing action and exterior spaces" in cop and private-eye shows. The power of its long-form narrative, however, is to explore character as it evolves over time, and in its demanding, branching stories of crime, injustice, marriage and family. As the show progresses, performers age visibly before the watching audience, and the viewers' knowledge of their histories and their interconnections inform every subsequent scene. It is important to recognize that movies cannot replicate this sort of aggregate intimacy and understanding between characters and audience. Ultimately, the long-form television narrative provides the audience with an experience that is closer to their experience of reality than a movie ever could.

Today, because of the internet and emerging technologies, new patterns of attention are arising. What looks like a transition from one era of storytelling to another is not only followed but also driven by changes in audience behavior.[11] These new patterns are bringing up new questions: for instance, how will binge viewing change the way we structure stories?[12] The writers of the aforementioned *House of Cards* apparently approached the storytelling as a 13-hour movie – this also means less reliance on traditional end-of-episode cliff-hangers to keep audiences thinking about the story until next week's episode. It is, however, interesting that they chose to create 13 episodes, which is the classic number of cable TV series episodes in one season. Another interesting case of a Netflix production is *Arrested Development*. Its creator, Mitch Hurwitz, has written the 15 new episodes commissioned by Netflix as the same moment in time seen from a different perspective in each episode. Freed from the old concepts of attention, he originally suggested that audiences could view them in any order, but then indicated that certain jokes wouldn't "pay off" unless you viewed them in the order they were created. This is probably just the beginning of the kind of experimentation we'll see as online platforms commission stories which are not only free from scheduled viewing but perhaps also designed around the new patterns of attention. It will be interesting to see how other patterns, such as pledging, which is connected with crowdfunding, so based on even more complex relationships between the audience and the storytellers, will influence storytelling.

For the moment, however, and for the purposes of this book, it will suffice to point out that as watching habits evolve, TV series tend more and more to be conceived and written as a long movie. Looking at series in this way, one could argue that in the course of the average American cable TV season of 13 episodes, the storytelling potential of the 90–120 minute length of a feature film has jumped 13 times. This has enabled the storytelling model to shift from the two-hour film to the scale of 19th-century novels such as those of Dickens, Balzac and Stendhal, where the complexity of plot and character development and the story world – as well as the broader canvas of milieu – peaked. Charles Dickens' novels are often referenced by film and TV critics in this context, as they first appeared in magazines in serialized form, a popular format at the time –in much the same way that a story evolves over the course of a series in television drama today.

As will become evident in the conversations in this book, today's TV writers also think of their shows and develop their stories and characters, using the season or even the whole series as dramatic unity. Sometimes they even refer to them as "visual novels," where the first episodes of the show have to be considered much as the first chapters of a book. "Think about the first few chapters of any novel you ever liked, say, Moby-Dick," writes David Simon in his book on *The Wire*.[13] "In the first couple chapters, you don't meet the whale, you don't meet Ahab, you don't even go aboard the Pequod. All that happens is you go with Ishmael to the inn and find out he has to share a room with some tattooed character. Same thing here. It's a visual novel."

Interestingly enough, in recent years scholars and critics have increasingly used the term "quality TV" to describe TV series which have attracted particular critical claim. This implies that some TV shows are of higher quality than others, which is, of course, a purely subjective evaluation and therefore has little academic merit. Robert J. Thompson attempted a definition of the term in his 1997 book *Television's Second Golden Age: From Hill Street Blues to ER*, which actually precedes the creation of the series now often described as "quality TV": "It must break the established rules of television and be like nothing that has come before. It is produced by people of quality aesthetic ancestry, who have honed their skills in other areas, particularly film. It attracts a quality audience. It succeeds against the odds, after initial struggles. It has large

ensemble cast, which allows for multiple plot lines. It has memory, referring back to previous episodes and seasons in the development of plot.
It defies genre classification. It tends to be literary. It contains sharp
social and cultural criticisms with cultural references and allusions to
popular culture. It tends toward the controversial. It aspires toward realism. Finally, it is recognized and appreciated by critics, winning awards
and critical acclaim."[14]

Another interesting term which emerged in the 2000s is Kristin
Thompson's "art television" – derived from the more familiar term "art
cinema," which also presupposes subjective evaluation. Thompson in
particular compares David Lynch's film *Blue Velvet* with his television
series *Twin Peaks* and argues that US television shows which are "art
television," such as *Twin Peaks*, have "a loosening of causality, a greater
emphasis on psychological or anecdotal realism, violations of classical
clarity of space and time, explicit authorial comment, and ambiguity."[15]
Thompson claims that series such as *Buffy the Vampire Slayer*, *The Sopranos*, and *The Simpsons* "have altered long-standing notions of closure
and single authorship," which means that "television has wrought its
own changes in traditional narrative form," while *The Simpsons* use a
"flurry of cultural references, intentionally inconsistent characterization, and considerable self-reflexivity about television conventions and
the status of the programme as a television show."

Whether we adopt one or both of the terms suggested above or indeed
propose new ones such as "long cinematic narrative," which admittedly
also does not escape the dangers of subjective evaluation (who shall
define what is cinematic?), one thing is clear: the TV series from the
third act of American TV history that we are mostly discussing in this
book seem to have common characteristics that can also be found in
films of alternative structure – as opposed to films of classic structure
or, in Thompson's words, "traditional narrative forms." They are, for
instance, characterized by multi-protagonist stories which overcome the
hierarchical organization reflected in our classic storytelling's privileg-
ing of one character and his or her point of view over the rest (multiple
narrative threads, large ensemble of characters) by the replacement of
the principle of causality with the principle of synchronicity (elimina-
tion of formalist explications for cause and effect, violations of classical
clarity and unity of time and space, ambiguity), and by a programmatic
desire to represent emotional truth, however complex it may prove to
be (realism, ambiguity, defiance of genre classification).

Perhaps writing for the screen is the literary form that corresponds
most to how we perceive the world today, and perhaps the TV screen
and its long narrative are the best expression of such perception. Indeed,

in the last decade or two, the great explosion of cinematic narrative complexity seems to be gravitating more and more towards TV and less towards the movies – possibly, among other reasons, because there are only so many threads and subtleties you can introduce into a two-hour film, but also because TV is traditionally more of a writer's medium and so perhaps more of a home to sophisticated writing.[16]

One cannot stress this enough: to ignore TV drama is to ignore one of the most important modes of storytelling of our time. To study story as it is practiced in TV drama, both creatively and analytically, one surely has to look deep into the creative processes of its writers as well as into the nature of their collaboration. The conversations I am including here, in the chronological order in which they took place over the last two years, cover quite a wide range of topics. What emerges is a treasury of invaluable insights into some of the many ways to write an American TV series – and some similarities and recurring themes that I will discuss in detail in my concluding reflections. Now the show belongs to the writers of some amazing work: the floor is theirs.

Conversations

Terence Winter

Terence Winter was a writer and executive producer for the HBO television series *The Sopranos* and is the creator, writer and executive producer of the HBO series *Boardwalk Empire*. Previously he wrote for *The Great Defender*, as well as the series *Sister, Sister; Xena: Warrior Princess; The Cosby Mysteries; The New Adventures of Flipper; Diagnosis: Murder; Charlie Grace; DiResta* and *The PJs*. He also wrote the screenplay for the 2005 film *Get Rich or Die Tryin'* and its accompanying video game, *50 Cent: Bulletproof*, as well as wrote and was a producer of the film *Brooklyn Rules* and the writer of *The Wolf of Wall Street*, directed by Martin Scorsese. He has won four Emmys, four WGA awards, a Golden Globe and an Edgar.

So why do you think that American TV has so much better writing right now than American movies?

Because in TV it's your own show, which is to say the writer's show, whereas in movies writers are often cut out of the process after the script is handed in. What really pisses me off is how in the movies, when the writer is not present, people mess around with the script. It's as if you draw up architectural plans for a house and a builder comes around when you're not there, and they just look at some pillars, for instance, and say, I don't like these. And they take them out without asking why you put them there. So you can't say, these pillars are important; if you remove them the second floor will collapse. Or, in writing terms, that scene or line of dialogue is important because it pays off in minute 92 of the film. Or then, sometimes, people will judge a script from the treatment, which is like trying to judge a cake by its recipe. You have to

11

eat the real thing first. Let me bake the cake, then you can tell me if you like it.

But why is it only on TV that it is the writer's show? Why not in the movies?

Because of TV's beginnings. It came from radio, which was mostly written by playwrights, so the creative process stayed in the writers' hands. The first sitcom was *The Goldbergs* in 1948, which was a radio play first.[1] While cinema started as being more about the visuals – plus it was silent, without spoken dialogue.

Can you say something about your background? Where did you learn, where did you start?

I was born into a working-class family in Brooklyn. And I was trained to be an auto mechanic – but then I decided to go to college. So I took a student loan and went on to study political science and journalism at NYU. In order to make a living, I took a job as a doorman, so I worked at night and studied during the day. But very soon, I realized I wouldn't be able to make a living that easily as a journalist. The first job offer I got was for less money than I made as a doorman. So I asked myself, who gets paid a lot of money? The only two "important" sounding jobs I was aware of were doctor and lawyer. That's how I decided to go to law school. I studied for years, passed the bar exam. By now I owed $73,000 in student loans, which in 1988 was like having a home mortgage. Then I considered becoming an Assistant District Attorney in Brooklyn, but that job paid only slightly more than my job as a doorman, so I couldn't afford to take it. That's it, I thought, I've educated myself into poverty. So I took a job with a large Manhattan law firm. It paid well, I had a fancy office, I would one day make partner...I had everything I thought I wanted. And I was bored to death.

So you suddenly realized that you had been chasing the wrong dream?

(nods) I was miserable. I spent my evenings at the movies, trying to forget the bad choices I had made. I was almost 30 by now, that age which is so pivotal in life, your last chance to change route. I loved the movies. I grew up watching movies and half-hour sitcoms. *The Bowery Boys*,[2] *The Honeymooners*...Channel 11 in New York. And I thought about breaking into Hollywood. But I had no idea how I would do that. My dream seemed unreachable. Still, I decided to try my hand at writing by performing my own stand-up comedy. I took a class and performed at The Comic Strip, worked the open mikes. Then went on to Catch a Rising Star a few times.[3] I never once considered pursuing that as a career, I just wanted to see if I could write jokes that worked. It's a tough path – have you seen that documentary about Joan Rivers, the comedy icon, *A Piece of Work?* She was a pivotal figure in a long line of female comics starting with Sophie Tucker. That film tells it all. But anyway, I found out that yes, I could at least write jokes that made people laugh and thought I could write a half-hour sitcom script. So I gave up every-thing and took a plane to Los Angeles. How crazy is that? You educate yourself for 20 years and then you start again from scratch, at something you have no freaking idea about.

Perhaps sometimes you have to risk stuff to get stuff?

(laughs) I guess so. At least in L.A., I did not become a doorman to make a living. But I needed a simple job, one which would only occupy me from nine to five, so I could spend the rest of the day trying to break into the movies – or into TV, in my case.

So how did you manage to break in?

I went to the Writers Guild library, read whatever scripts I could get my hands on, (laughs) I sometimes stole them and brought them home to photocopy them. I studied them to find out how they were struc-tured. Then I wrote one spec script after the other. A *Cheers* spec, a *Seinfeld* spec. And I learned about the Catch-22 of the Hollywood sys-tem. I could not get a job without an agent and I could not get an agent without a job. Trying to figure out what to do, I made a promise to myself that I would do something to further my writing career every day. Each night before I went to bed, I would ask myself, "What did you do today to make your writing career happen?", and if I had noth-ing to offer, I would get out of bed and write something or mail out a script or anything which could qualify as a valid answer to that ques-tion. At some point I got a list of agents from the WGA. I would call, send scripts and never get an answer – there were just too many people looking for agents. One day I saw a name on the lists, which I recog-nized as the name of someone I went to law school with in New York. I called him up. "No", he said, "I am not a literary agent, I am a real estate attorney, it's just that a client of mine wrote a book and I had to register the rights so I did that and got bonded as an agent." "Okay", I said, "I don't care whether you know anything about this or not, from now on, you are my agent." I created a letterhead, set up a voicemail system, got a post office box, everything. I basically created a phony agency, then put my spec scripts in manila envelopes and I would go from production company to production company as a messenger and deliver the scripts which were supposedly sent from that agency, which did not really exist. I was the writer, his agent and the agent's messenger all at the same time. And I was the agent's assistant too. One Friday afternoon the phony agency got a message from the executive producer of *The Fresh Prince of Bel Air*, who had read my scripts and was interested in having me in to pitch some ideas. I was bummed because it was already 4 p.m. in Los Angeles and my agent friend in New York was already gone for the weekend, so I'd have to wait until Monday for them to connect. But then I realized that since he didn't know anything about being an agent, I could call her back and pretend I was him. We had a nice conversation and she asked if I had any other "younger" material since *Fresh Prince* was a teenage-oriented show. I lied and told her "my client" had just written a terrific *Wonder Years* spec, which was a lie – at that point I had given her everything I had. So I told her I could get it to her by Tuesday and she agreed. So from Friday night until Tuesday afternoon, I cranked out a *Wonder Years* spec, then threw my baseball hat on and delivered it to the *Fresh Prince* offices.

You're an amazing storyteller, anybody ever told you that? (laugh) So what happened then? When was it anyway?

It was in 1993. A few weeks later I got to pitch them some ideas, which was my first real foot in the door.

And, 17 years later, here you are, with Boardwalk Empire, *your first own show. What was the inspiration for that?*

As I was winding down on *The Sopranos*, an executive from HBO gave me the book *Boardwalk Empire*, which is essentially a history of Atlantic City written by Nelson Johnson. She asked me to read it and see if I thought there was a TV series in it. And then, almost as an afterthought, she told me that Martin Scorsese was attached to it. I told her in that case I didn't even need to read it, that if Scorsese was involved, I would *absolutely* find a TV series in the book, which I did. It all started with one chapter, which covered the Prohibition era.

And the story of that one chapter is what you then turned into the arc of the first season. But what carries each season? And do you think of this as something which will go on for many seasons?

It's one season at a time for me, really. Once I read the book and I knew that Nucky was going to be the center of our universe, it was first a question of creating the characters around him and then creating a dilemma for him for Season One. I knew the series was going to start the day the

Prohibition was enacted, I knew it would have something to do with alcohol, and the whole idea that the world was rapidly changing. The dramatic rise in crime, the types of crime that actually gave rise to (as we say in the show) a new breed of criminal – you know, people who were willing to kill each other for fast money. Suddenly, overnight, alcohol was a tremendously valuable commodity and that meant people were killing and dying over it. So in Nucky, I had a character who was a corrupt politician whose life was about to change dramatically, as he ran a city situated on the ocean, which was the source for all this alcohol. It was too good for him to pass up, it was too powerful. He knew he could make millions of dollars by trafficking in this illegal substance and he had to commit to that – but as a result his life would change, because, again, this was going to be very violent. So that was sort of the idea that gave birth to Season One. Now, how to dramatize that? You know, he has a protégé who is back from the war, who is sort of disillusioned and violent, he's been a soldier for three years and he's back and wants to make a lot of money and is ambitious and gets involved with an alcohol deal that goes south – and in that he has consequences that reverberate throughout the season.

The story is very much reminiscent of the movies of the 70s, don't you think?

Sure, I grew up watching them. But really, writing is all a question of finding conflict. I read a book on writing once that put it in very simple terms – there was a drawing of a stick figure man on one side and on the other side there was a drawing of the sun, which represented his goal. And in between the two there were several straight lines, which represented the obstacles to that goal. That is in the very simplest terms what we do, finding out what the character wants and creating obstacles to him or her getting it. Nucky's goal is to peacefully run Atlantic City and make millions of dollars, so we ask ourselves, what are the challenges he faces? The government is trying to shut him down, the Prohibition agents are after him, his protégée engages in this horrible massacre that ends up being a political disaster for him, the woman that he becomes enamored of has a husband who abuses her and he murders him, so that becomes a complicated relationship for him . . . and so on.

How many plotlines do you have per episode?

There is no rule, but it's usually two or three, I'd say. There was an episode where we had seven different storylines going on. That was Episode Ten in Season One, called "The Emerald City." That means a lot of juggling. What we do in that writers' room is talk for three months trying to unravel the plots for the season and how things unfold. It's a lot of deciding how much information to give out and at what particular time and where it is most effective to introduce that information. How much and when are really the two big questions of telling a story. It's almost like cooking. You stir in the ingredients and you taste the result and you say, it needs a little more of this and a little more of that, and you sort of almost do it by instinct. I've been doing this long enough, so I know when I read a script or watch an episode how it flows and how the story moves and whether it needs to move quicker, or if you need more information, or it's time to get back to that other story now, we've spent enough time here, we need to visit the subplot... That kind of thing.

When you communicate with each other, like in the writers' room, do you use terms like "acts" and "turning points"?

No. Because we don't have commercial breaks, it's less focused on acts. In network TV, because there is going to be a commercial here and there, it's going to be broken up into little chunks, like a six-act structure, which is kind of weird. I mean, stories have a beginning, a middle and an end, that's really the only structure there is. So we just really think of it in those terms. There is a problem, the problem gets more complicated and then there is a resolution to that problem. That's really how we talk about it.

There are personal lines which go through a whole season; which means that as an audience you cannot watch them in a different chronological order than the one they were written in. You have to watch the whole season as if you were watching a twelve-hour movie. Is that how you think of it, as a long movie?

We try to make each episode stand alone, as if it's one mini-movie, so when you just happen to watch this one it still has its own beginning, middle and end, and it makes sense. It's like one chapter in a book, I look at it that way. But to really appreciate it you have to watch the whole thing, you really want to read the whole thing. This is a funny thing with reviewers, when they react to a few episodes. There's so much more, I mean, there's something happening in Episode Two, which will pay off in Episode Nine, that they're not aware of yet. And they might say, "I don't understand the point of that scene, who cares about that guy?" To which I say, "Be patient, we know what we're doing." Everything is there for a reason and if you come back at the end of the season and that thing didn't mean anything, now your point is valid. But after a few episodes it's too early to make a declaration like that. But the other thing is, not everything has to mean something – sometimes life is like that. You meet a person and then they're gone. Not everyone has a big impact on your life. You run into people and you have an interesting little encounter – and they go away, never to be seen again. That happens with TV characters too, and it's okay.

Yes, but we strive to find meaning in everything.

(laughs) Yes, we do. Plus the audience is trained to expect the big pay-off. You know, from years and years of watching movies and TV, they are, very sadly, very familiar with a particular formula, so they can't believe that you will possibly introduce a problem and then not give them a clear-cut resolution to it. That drives them crazy. And even after years of watching *The Sopranos*, where we were almost famous for not spoon-feeding the audience the ending they expected, people still insisted, "Oh no, I bet they're gonna tell us what happened." And very often we wouldn't and we'd drive people crazy. They still expected it though.

You do like that, don't you, to provoke the audience and educate them in different ways? Go against what they expect?

Yes, as a matter of fact, I do. Unfortunately, what they expect a lot of times is really not good. It's sort of the easy way out, it doesn't require any thought. It doesn't require the audience to think or ask questions. And that is not satisfying to me as a storyteller. You may want every-thing wrapped up neatly in a bow, but sometimes the best stories leave you wondering what they meant. You wonder what happened to the characters after they cut to black or after the screen froze, as opposed to having them ride off into the sunset together. Look at the end of *The Graduate*, which goes out on these very uncertain looks between this couple. If you made that movie today you would have to say if they lived happily ever after or not – but as it is, you wonder where that relationship went.

To Kramer vs. Kramer, *I guess.*

(laughs) Yes, probably.

Do you plan this, for yourself, as something which is going to go on for six seasons?

Yes, well, I hope so. I have to think that way, in order to come up with the stories I'm coming up with now. I'm working under the assumption that this is a series that will go on for five or six years. Six seasons of 12 episodes. In my own head that is what it is. If I knew we only had two years I would start writing towards the conclusion now, I would try to wrap up the story in some way or another. Doesn't mean that you have to kill everybody, not everyone has to die, but you have to figure out a way to come to a satisfying conclusion for the stories told so far.

Do you plan to use the time frame of Prohibition?

It can go to the crash of 1929, where we had devastating financial consequences for the world, or to the end of Prohibition in 1933, which would be a logical time too. As the series began with Prohibition it could end with its repeal, but that would require me to jump ahead quite a bit. If we only had six years, for example, I'd have to jump ahead several years at one point. Now, we are coming back in Season Two and it's only a few months later. So it would require some very big jumps as we go on.

How much do you care about authenticity?

A lot, we're extremely detail-oriented. And still people think we make mistakes when we haven't. There was a book called *Public Speaking and Influencing Men in Business* by Dale Carnegie, who used to teach public speaking classes, and up until 1922 or '23 he spelled his name (he spells it) C-a-r-n-a-g-e-y. Then he realized that people, when they heard his name, thought he was related to Andrew *Carnegie*, who was a billionaire industrialist, but that was a different spelling, so he changed the spelling of his name in 1924 to match the billionaire's name, because he thought people would think they were related. But that was later. In 1920 he still spelled it the other way. At one point one of our characters says, I'm taking a Dale Carnagey class, and he has the book in his hand. So when the time came to film this, I said, "I don't care if people think it's wrong, let's just stick to the right way and let people learn or not learn." And of course people on the internet wrote, "They screwed up, they spelled the name wrong, don't they check these things . . . " But we were right.

Will you walk me through the development of one episode? Do you define the core story on your own and then take it to the writers' room?

I come in at the beginning of the season with the broad strokes, where the whole season is going to go for each of the different characters. I start with the characters and what their journey is going to be, for example Nucky in Season One: we meet him, he meets Mrs. Schroeder, he makes a deal with Arnold Rothstein to import some alcohol, the deal goes bad, he realizes it's his protégée Jimmy who did the deal, he needs to frame somebody, he frames Margaret's husband and he solves the problem by the end of Episode One. But he has a bigger problem, because now he is in a war with Arnold Rothstein and he's also caught the eye of a federal Prohibition agent. In Episode Two, the Prohibition agent comes to meet him, Nucky needs to buy off Mrs. Schroeder, pays her some money, hoping that she won't say anything about her husband not being involved in alcohol, and it turns out at the end of that episode that one of the victims from Jimmy's massacre actually lived. Now we're into Episode Three, and it gets more complicated. The feds get some information from this guy that Jimmy might be involved, so now Nucky needs to send Jimmy out of town. By Episode Four Nucky becomes closer with Margaret Schroeder, by Episode Five they actually sleep together, by Episode Six they move in together. All this I've defined in the very beginning, but specifically how it all comes to happen I don't really know. All I know is they'll get together, their relationship gets a little rocky, the brother gets shot, it just sort of goes along from there. And again, it is just very sketchy ideas of how it ends up developing. He has an external threat to his kingdom and by Episode 12 he solves everything, he makes a deal with Arnold Rothstein to get out of the problem he had in the pilot, and it all wraps up. Once we have the big arc, we sit down to beat out the episodes, scene by scene. Like, this is what we are trying to achieve in this episode and what happens specifically is...For example, in Episode Four Nucky and Margaret Schroeder have a moment where she gets a little bit involved in his world, so we ask ourselves, how might that happen. Well, if he had a party of some sort and he asks her to come to it, like Cinderella, and she comes to be with him...So what if it was his birthday party? Okay, but why would she come to his birthday party, well, she's there to deliver something, okay, so what would she be delivering? Oh, what if she got a new job in a dress shop and she is asked to come and deliver a dress? Well, why would she deliver a dress at a birthday party? His girlfriend is there and we've already seen that she knows this woman is a potential rival, and then she comes to deliver a dress and while she's there Nucky dances with her, she has that little taste of being with the King, what that's like, and she realizes she really wants to be part of this world...So you know, it starts to slowly come together. And once we've all agreed on how the story will play out, we write it into an outline and then one of us is assigned to go off and write that script.

Are all of the writers producers also?

Well, most of the writer/producers you see listed on a TV show are mainly writing; a lot of them aren't actually producing. But when they are, it's in the creative sense. Someone at Howard Korder's level *is* producing[4] – he'll go to casting, he'll take part in all of our creative meetings, he'll be on set. In terms of writers having producers' titles, it is mostly a way to develop a hierarchy in the writing staff. Staff writer, story editor, executive story editor, co-producer, producer, supervising producer, co-executive producer, executive producer – it's a way to delineate the level at which you are functioning, it's more and more in terms of rank, like ranks in the military, from private to general. It's a raise in pay, it's a raise in responsibility, it's an acknowledgment of the fact that you've been in the business for a long time, that you have more of a track record and also a way to delineate who is doing what.

Is it your decision which writer to assign which episode?

Yes. If anybody has a particular affinity for a story, I might assign that one to them, for example if it was an area they originally pitched. If that affinity is there I usually defer to that, so I say, you seem excited about this, why don't you take a shot at that episode.

So what happens after the first draft is in?

I give notes on the first draft and the writer will take another pass on it. Generally, there is one more draft and a set of notes and at that point I'll take the script and do my pass through it. So I will usually begin my work on it at the third draft.

So you will do the third and final draft of all episodes. How much, would you say, do you change?

It depends. I had situations where I changed everything, so I rewrote it from word one, and some episodes that I only changed a little. Howard Korder's scripts are generally shot as written – if anything, I'll do some editing for length. But generally I do some rewriting on every script, some more than others. But I consider it my job as the showrunner and head writer, that everything will get filtered through me anyway and the idea of taking credit for it...I'll only put my name on scripts that I write in their entirety from the beginning. You know, people are split about how they feel about it. There are showrunners who feel that if they rewrite more than 50% of a script, they're gonna put their name on it. And that's totally valid. I choose to not do that, I choose to just sort of say, this is my job and whoever was assigned the script initially, their name stays on it. I am not interested in taking more credit but I certainly understand why people would be.

How is that different for a writer than what she experiences in the movies, when a director will very easily rewrite a script just to make it their own, as they call it? And what is it for you, this need for rewriting? Is it about having a different taste from the original writer? I guess you have been rewritten as well.

Yes, I've been rewritten, but I think it is different in a series than in a movie. In a series you need to feel that it's one cohesive piece of writing, that it's the same voice telling the story. So what I look for is, does this episode sound like the other episode, do the characters sound different, does he still sound like Nucky and is the tone and the flow of the episode similar? I mean, the reason why I filter it through myself is so that it feels like the same television series throughout. It will be different stories and different subject matters but it needs to feel consistent in the way the story is told and the voice it is told in. And ultimately, you are right, that is just my taste, I'm the one who decides what this show is and if I'm right or wrong, for better or worse… (laughs) Hopefully I'm making these scripts better, I think I am, while working on them. Someone ultimately has to decide what is this show. In movies it is different. Several years ago I was rewritten by a director who in my opinion absolutely destroyed the script I wrote. It was a script I was very proud of, it was greenlit[5] immediately by the studio, in fact the studio head said, this script is so great, all we need is a director, and we'll start shooting this on Monday morning. The director they hired rewrote it to a point where it made absolutely no sense. He took a script that everybody loved and unfortunately I think really ruined it. And the movie was a huge failure. The thing that was frustrating was that it was done really without consultation, without considering what was there beforehand, it felt like it was somebody just trying to put their stamp on it. What was insulting about it is he never asked me to explain to him why this scene is here and what does this mean, before he went on to change it. And he made all these changes that didn't have any reason to be made, which did not serve the story properly, and, again, it was done without asking me. Again, it is as if you give the architectural plans to a house to a builder, and they ignore your plans and just start putting things where they want them to be, put pillars where they don't belong or take the support pillars away, without asking you, the architect, why was this here in the first place, or at least giving you your day in court to say, this is why I did this, rather than simply saying, I want to make this my own. And what you're gonna make in this way is a house that doesn't really work. You know, a second storey that is going to collapse.

That is what happens very often in movies and certainly in the case of that movie. It was a shame because I was really proud of the original script, the studio greenlit it immediately and then it was taken apart by a director...

It hurt.

Yes.

What about your moral rights?

I tried to appeal to the studio but that was a weird situation because at the time they were in flux, there was nobody really in charge, the studio head was on his way out, they didn't have a strong producer on the movie. And it was also a case of, you know, we have a highly acclaimed director, and nobody at the studio wants to be the person who says you have to listen to the writer, nobody wanted to take that responsibility. Everybody privately agreed with me. Everybody knew that I wasn't just being a precious writer trying to protect my material. Everybody knew what was happening. But nobody wanted to take the responsibility.

Were you shown his final draft?

Oh, yeah. I was shown it while it was happening. And I was desperately trying to ride this ship and it was really dead ears. At the eleventh hour the studio got on board and tried to appeal to the director to go back to my original version but it didn't work. He had his vision of what he wanted to do and they ultimately, rather than fight that battle, just allowed him to do it and the result is the movie you see.

Did you pull your name back?

I didn't, for business reasons. If you're awarded full credit, very often there is a clause in your contract where you get a bonus, financially. If I took my name off then I wouldn't have gotten that bonus, so for financial reasons I needed to keep my name on it.

Did he get a writing credit?

No. He tried to get one, which was another insult, and one of the things his reps said early on was that he "always takes a writing credit" in his movies. I mean, you don't *take* a writing credit, you are given the writing credit by the Writers Guild, you don't take anything! He was more than willing to attempt to get one, but as much as he rewrote my script, the core elements of the story are still the same. I knew he wasn't going to get it if he tried, but I was certainly not going to give it to him because he decided to rewrite my script because he felt like it. The whole thing was an insult and it was very emblematic of the difference between television and film. And it was a perfect example of why films get ruined so very often.

Sadly it is also a very common experience for a writer in the film industry so it is helpful to address all aspects here, especially as the writer's role is so very different in TV. Why do you think it is that they don't wise up? There is so much successful storytelling on TV, one would think they would wonder why? I mean, there is a lot of predictable storytelling in movies at the moment.

I think a lot of it is lowest common denominator storytelling. They take these very simple stories, a lot of them are very clichéd, comic book action movies that play all over the world, that translate into any other language. So things like nuance or character development or cultural differences do not exist, you almost don't need dialogue, it's all about the visuals, it's all about explosions, very simple good guy bad guy, you know, this guy doesn't like that guy, or this person is in love with that person, and it is a very easy story to tell, and it translates easily all over the world.

It looks like at the moment there is very little independent filmmaking in America.

Yes, very little. When I see a movie get made that is actually a character drama, I go, "Wow, thank god someone financed this movie" or I wonder how it got made, who paid for it. Think about what the big movies of the 70s were. The big box office movies in the 70s were *French Connection, Dog Day Afternoon, Midnight Cowboy*. These were the films that were big, big Hollywood movies. They would be considered independent cinema today.

What was character drama then is what is in television today.

Yes, thank god there is television. You are right, it is much, much closer to the cinema of the 70s than the Hollywood movies of today.

And that is because TV production is writer-led. So why won't they wise up?

It's about money, making movies is a business and business comes first. And as long as they are making hundreds of millions of dollars, they do not care about the story. If they're gonna have a movie like *Iron Man 3* make half a billion dollars worldwide, it doesn't matter if it's a well made film, or, you know, *GI Joe* or *Transformers*, movies that are just devoid of any kind of character development – but those movies make a fortune. So, if you are in the business of making money, they almost can't afford to not make these movies.

But American TV is also selling all over the world with great success.

That is true, yes. By March, *Boardwalk Empire* will be all over the world.

And probably millions have already watched it on pirated copies or illegal downloads.

(laughs) I'm sure they have.

Have there been situations, either on this series, or on series you have worked on before, where an episode went completely wrong and the writer had to go? Or would the showrunner just rewrite it?

The showrunner would just rewrite it. I mean, there are people who get let go from writing staffs. If I get two scripts in a row from the same writer that I have to completely rewrite, then it's not working out. Not every writer is right for every show. Not every director is right for every show, not every actor is right for every show. So that is not necessarily an indication that the person is a bad writer, they're just not the right fit for the show. I would hope that the writer at least gets me 50% there. Give me a draft, which is halfway to where I need it to be. Ideally it would be 95%. But when they miss the mark so completely that I need to rewrite it from the first page, then it's usually an indication that this is not gonna work.

When you were not a showrunner but a staff writer, do you remember living with the fear that what you deliver is not going to be good enough?

Sure. Yeah. You're doing your best. You're really trying to mimic the showrunner's idea of what the series is. With any luck, you have a story and an outline that makes sense. Or it is not a good story and it is your job to make it make sense, when you go off to write that script. You know, showrunners are very busy. David Chase, for example: I knew the last thing he wanted to do was take a phone call from one of his writers saying, "Can you talk with me about this scene?" So it really was up to me to figure out how to make the script work. If it didn't make sense, then fix it, without changing what's there. The outline is written and he wants to see a certain thing, that's what he expects to get back. You just have to hope that your vision of what the show is comports with his vision of what the show is. And that it feels like the same series. I was lucky enough on *The Sopranos* to have figured out early on what it was that David (Chase) wanted and what those characters sounded like.

So how is the experience you described with the film director different from having the same experience with a showrunner?

The difference is a head writer or showrunner is actually a writer. The film director I referred to earlier was in my opinion not a writer. And there was a lack of respect. I think the showrunner-writer for the most part would at least sit down with you and try to figure out what it was that you wrote and why you wrote it that way. The film director just tossed out the script without any consideration. That was where the problem was. If you're gonna write something at least have a discussion with the original writer or explain to me why you think what was there did not work. What was wrong with what we had. There were never any of those discussions, it was just sort of done very haphazardly.

Is it a matter of ego?

Of course.

As a staff writer on a TV show did you ever have the feeling that something was rewritten in the wrong direction or was even destroyed by a head writer?

Yes. I've been on some sitcoms, which are a different type of writing because they're often written by tremendous staffs, sort of written by committee. I've been on sitcoms where a writer would turn in a draft of his script and it's very funny, and the way the process works is, we'll table the script. Everybody at the writers' table will read the script, and there'll be a joke. Then someone asks "Do we have a better joke than this?" And if you say this to a group of 12 comedy writers, then every one of them thinks they have a better joke and they will start pitching. And with comedy, because you've read this thing five times already, it's not as funny the fifth time as it was the first time. Somebody pitches a new joke that you haven't heard and you think, "Oh yeah, let's use that instead." You go through the whole script and you end up replacing 90% of it. So, if you are the original writer, by the time you film it, there is really almost none of your work there anymore. And it's not necessarily that what is there now is better, very often it is just a lateral move. It gets rewritten for no other real reason than it was something to do. For me it was really unsatisfying. It wasn't so much that I felt they are ruining my script, it was more like my script was just as good when I handed it in as what we had at the end, so I don't know why we didn't stick with it and make it work.

Do you have the final cut?

I make the final determination of what the episode should look and sound like. I don't know that I have that contractual right; probably I don't. I think if HBO wanted to come in and force me to cut a certain scene, they could probably do that legally. But they haven't ever done that.

What are the times when they actually communicate with you?

They read the outlines of the scripts, they call me and have questions about them, suggestions, ask for clarification about story points.

When you say HBO you mean ... ?

The president of HBO and his creative team. So it's four executives that read the outlines and comment on them. And then they read scripts, they watch the daily footage of the actors, they see how things are looking and what the actors sound like, just to make sure that things are good the way they are going. Then they watch the cuts of the episodes. Yeah, they are in pretty constant contact.

They are like gatekeepers. You have to go through a gate guarded by four people to get to the audience.

Yes, and I guess they guard that gate even more closely if they think there is a problem. When they think things are in good hands, they back away. As long as you're responsible and you keep turning out things that are good, there's no problem. It's like running any business. They are the parent corporation and they have a lot of subsidiary businesses. Those businesses are the TV series. And if you are a subsidiary, if you're turning a profit, if it's well run and everybody seems happy and everything's on schedule, they don't need to supervise you so closely. If you were constantly going over budget and over schedule, there were reports of people not being happy on the set, scripts were late and things like that, then there would be a lot more scrutiny. And the end of the scrutiny is that they replace the person who is running the show, because it's a huge investment for them, and they've got to make sure that this thing is running right. Once you have a show like this, that's a solid hit, the idea is to keep it running for several years. So they really have a tremendous investment and need to make sure this thing continues to be successful.

How do you choose your writers and how do you choose your directors?

A lot of it is based on people I've worked with before, recommendations of people I've worked with before. Sometimes it's just a question of reading scripts that I like; that, in conjunction with a personal meeting. You know, sometimes the person may be a great writer but they're crazy and I don't know that I want to spend ten hours a day in a room with a crazy person, so there's something I call "hangability". If there's a person I want to hang out with every day, they are talented, they seem like they get the show, they have a good sense of humor, they don't seem crazy, if I can stay in the room with this person for ten hours a day, and not wanna strangle them … I ask myself, Will they work well with other people, are they collaborative and not too sensitive and do they want to share with me? What's really important to me is a willingness to open up about yourself, about your past, about things that have embarrassed you, weird stuff about yourself – you have to open up your veins and spill it out in the writers' room – because that's the stuff that we tell stories about. I would like to hear from you what's the most embarrassing thing that's ever happened to you.

Don't get me started.

(laughs) You know, what was it like when you had your heart broken? When you were terribly sad? What do you dream about? That's part of our job as writers, one has to be willing to access that and then share it with everybody else and put it on TV, and, if you are not willing to do this, then you are not helping me as the head writer, because that is what I need from you, I need you to bare your soul. And it's hard, it's like talking to a therapist but you are not talking to a therapist, you're talking to other writers and ultimately you are talking to millions of people, because your innermost thoughts are gonna be dramatized in TV episodes – but that's the job. Directors, same thing. I need a director who can shape that script and take it to another level. To tell that story visually and bring something to it that wasn't on the page, while still respecting what was on the page. Finding a way to dramatize this stuff in a visual way, get those actors to perform these scenes in the most plausible, dynamic way and also bear in mind that the entire series has to look like one person wrote and directed all of it.

Was it different at The Sopranos? *For instance, in* The Wire *they had different directors, even cinema directors, direct different episodes, to give each episode a distinctive look.*

We have the best TV director in the world, Tim Van Patten.

But he doesn't do every single episode.

I wish he could, but that would be physically impossible, because, while we are shooting one episode, we are prepping to shoot the next episode, so one director couldn't do it. And for the last week of a shoot you are out scouting locations, casting, etc. Tim did four of the first 12 (episodes) for us. And he is on set for the rest, to guide people as an executive producer. We've also had several directors of *The Sopranos* who worked with us, Allen Coulter, Alan Taylor, who need no supervision at all, and we also tried out some new people with whom we haven't worked before but who are very talented – Brian Kirk, Brad Anderson, Jeremy Podeswa, Simon Cellan-Jones – guys whose work I'd known but didn't know personally. But also on *The Sopranos* – each episode looked the same despite there being only one rule – the camera never moved in the therapy scenes. There was a wide shot and a close up and a medium shot, two sides, and that was it. There was no moving cameras and no pushing in, none of that stuff, but other than that... Because you don't want to look at a TV series and feel "This doesn't look like the same show, what's going on here?" There's a certain world depicted, at least that's my philosophy, and it should look like the same place every week.

When do you stop changing the script?

The script will keep changing up until and during the time we're shooting, and sometimes beyond that, in the sense that we'll add lines in looping. As we start scouting locations and we do scheduling, I might realize that a script will take 15 days to shoot while we want to shoot it in 12 days, so something has to change. So I either start cutting scenes or combining scenes or shortening scenes to get it to fit that schedule. Then we'll have our cast read through and I'll hear them read it aloud and I may say "Now that I hear the actors say this, I need to change this line." Even on the set, while we are filming it, I'll watch a scene and I'll say, "No, I'm not really sure that this is working, now that I see the scene on its feet, let's change this, and why don't you say this line first and come in and do that." Even in editing, I'll cut lines out. Now that I see it all together, I don't think we need that line. So it continues to change all the way out to the finished product.

Which shows how important it is that the writer is part of production. Perhaps this is part of the secret of success.

Very much so. You don't have this in movies.

What happens if you are in the editing room and there's a scene which you wrote and which you don't like any more, but Tim is of a different opinion?

We fight (laughs). No, we don't really fight. We debate. And we persuade each other. I respect him immensely and he knows that if he thinks differently of something I will give it a great deal of thought. But ultimately you have to go with your gut. It's very rare that we feel so strongly about something that we disagree. We do have the same sensibilities. So usually it is the other way around. It has happened that we both say the exact same joke at the same time. And we looked at each other and laughed because we just think alike. So, usually 95% of the time we agree exactly on how something should look or feel and in the few times we don't, it's not such a big deal so if he feels strongly about it, I'll usually say fine. Or vice versa.

This is a happy marriage.

(laughs) Yes, it is.

Warren Leight

Warren Leight has worked on *Law & Order: Criminal Intent* and was the showrunner of *In Treatment, Lights Out* and *Law & Order: Special Victims Unit*. Leight won Broadway's 1999 Tony award as author of Best Play for *Side Man*, which was also nominated for the Pulitzer Prize.

Let me start by saying that you seem to be one of the very few showrunners who are based in New York. Do you feel lonely?

(laughs) There are more shows being shot here now, but yes, most of the shows are still being written in Los Angeles. That's unfortunate. I think you can always tell the difference – in choice of locations or characters and the use you make of them. I would get scripts from my L.A. based writers and they would refer to some old Jewish character who hasn't appeared in New York in 30 years. They didn't understand the ever-changing ethnic patterns. There was a character, and we knew he was up for something bad because he was in Central Park at night. And the actors in New York called and said, you know, there's 200,000 people in there at night, bicycling and running, it's not what it used to be.

New York seems to have a great pool of actors.

I've been in NY theater for a long time, and for *Lights Out* we did 13 episodes, shot all of them in Queens, and the cast is terrific in every episode. And I maybe spend half an hour a week on casting; there's a very strong pool of actors here. I would call the casting director, tell her I need this type, ten years younger, and she would send me four guys and I'd look at them quickly on the computer and I would have what I want. In L.A., you're booking a job; here it's a commitment, both for crew and for cast.

Did you do Lights Out *and* In Treatment *at the same time?*

No, no, that would have been impossible. I did Season Two of *In Treatment,*[1] which was 35 episodes. It was partly based on the Israeli series but in fact we had to move away from it at some point.

Why is that? The Israeli series run out of episodes?

No. It was a little bit of a gift to come in and there were 35 pre-existing episodes. But you get more pressure as the season goes on and you are writing more and more quickly. As the season went on, the wheels fell off the wagon. They lost control of some of the stories. It was uneven in a way that would not be tolerated here. Four episodes in, he stopped going to therapy and his daughter came into his place and the big sub-plot was that she was a lesbian and the father had a hard time with that. She was going on a spiritual quest as many Israelis do, to India, it just wasn't anything we could use here. And the story was getting tougher and tougher. It turned out the Israeli writer didn't want to follow it through to its emotional conclusion, and I couldn't imagine getting us to spend four or five episodes with one character and then just switching like that, that's just not fair. So, I would change things like that. Another thing I tried to do with *In Treatment* was track each patient horizontally from one episode to the next, but track each patient each week, so crosshatching a little bit. And they hadn't done much of that. So I had the luxury of looking at what they did and then . . . it was almost like having 35 first drafts. And in some cases I discarded them. Some of the storylines wouldn't work here; I suppose in Israel there's all kinds of cultural connotations to a woman at 40 who hasn't had a child yet, but that's not the case here and you really can't write that here. You also can't end that storyline with the therapist saying, "Have the baby, that's the most important thing," which is how the Israeli storyline ended. It would also be wrong for a therapist to tell somebody that.

So what did you work from – the scripts or the films?

We watched the episodes. We had transliterations of the scripts. Then we had a writers' room for three weeks. The entire staff watched all the episodes and we re-blocked in broad strokes the characters' main arc and the therapist's arc for that week. So that before the scripts came in, we were already on a very different path. And then the other thing that happens on a show like that and probably on any other show too: as you shoot things change. And certainly in the therapist's session, the therapist might say, "I want her to realize that this week," but you have no control over where your patient is going to go. I have no control over where my actors are going to go emotionally. I may have pre-conceptions, I may have desires but that's a pretty intimate show and whatever was happening between the actors had to be reflected in the next episode even if . . . I kept praying for John Mahoney's character to break down and I kept beating him up and he wouldn't crack. And it was frustrating to Gabriel (Byrne) but it actually reflected what would happen if a 65 year old man who would never go to therapy starts to feel things – he would close up. The moment when Mahoney's character finally did break down was two and a half episodes later than I thought it would be. And it was very moving and it paved the season in a lot of ways. But it wouldn't have happened had I kept the original storyline where the character disappeared or had I forced the issue. Listening to the actors got us there.

You were showrunner on In Treatment, Lights Out *and before that on* Law and Order: Criminal Intent.

Yeah, back to back.

Did you work in a similar way on all three shows?

No. *Law and Order*[2] has a different approach. First of all it's much less character-based. It's a 45-beat murder mystery. It's one A line, sometimes a B line. So the best way to do that show is one hour with the writer breaking the story and it takes sometimes seven days to break a story on that show. The plotting is so complicated. I was on staff for four years and then a showrunner for two years. In those six years there was never one episode that the showrunner didn't beat out, with the writer. In other shows people come in with a pitch, but this is such a tightly plotted show and there were so many unwritten rules. Also it's the showrunner's duty in that show to make sure you're not repeating a beat. So if seven episodes ago a man who we think is a suspect could not have been a suspect because he was having an affair on his wife you can't be using that beat. You have to try and keep your storylines and you have to know your actors on that show. Somehow, a group cannot plot that tightly. It really never works. The most we ever had in a room plotting was three, in six years. It was a one-on-one show. You have to make it as hard as possible on your detectives, which means it's as hard as possible on your writers. You just keep trying and trying.

What about In Treatment?

I started out with one writer for each storyline. I beat out every writer's story after the writers' room met, we'd go over each storyline. I wanted an outline, I'd give notes on the outline, I wanted every episode to have a three-act structure. There's a risk of a show with two people in the room – it can be formless, it may not have a narrative thrust. I thought that was sometimes the case with the Israeli series. Even in Season One sometimes, someone would say, "I had a dream last night," and they would talk about the dream and that would eat up six minutes of the clock – and sometimes the dream wasn't even on point thematically with the episode. Usually a writer would give me one or two drafts, sometimes three drafts. Most of the rewriting I would have to do was of the therapist, his voice had to stay the same, and he treats his patients differently but we have to understand his character. Mostly the writers are focused on their patient and they identify with their patient, so it fell on me to protect Gabriel's character. Also, Gabriel is sitting in that chair 12 hours a day. I had to keep him engaged. In real life, therapists don't have as many deductions and don't have as many highlights. Every session doesn't end with a great moment for the therapist. But I had a world class actor on that show who needed to be challenged or on some level I would end up losing him.

So each writer has one patient, so four episodes more or less?

Yes. We shot every episode in two days, which is very little. So every week I needed three new episodes to get published – that's the word they use. But also in the morning, I was on set every morning with Gabriel, it was the first time he would look at the morning script that was being shot. We read through it, usually the other actor was prepared so we could begin the shooting on the patient's side, but we'd read through for an hour, talk about it with Gabriel. The actors would go to makeup, the lighting would begin, and I would go upstairs every morning and do a rewrite of the first half of that episode, as fast as I could. Adjusting to what I'd seen take place. That was my responsibility. I seldom had the writer who wrote that episode do that. Partly because they're attached to what they wrote and your job as a showrunner is to have the sense of what is possible to do or what can get done. The original writer has a script in his head but Gabriel doesn't hear it that way. Maybe if you had four weeks to rehearse a play, and I had a lot of playwrights on that show, I could get them there. But if you're shooting in an hour you have to meet the actors more than halfway sometimes. And you have to trust their instincts. At some point Gabriel would know his character better than the writers did. Better than I did. So I just watched him and sensed when he was uncomfortable. If I noticed he glitched, I wanted to know what was that, or he would ask me a question, he'd say, "Why is the character saying this?" I'd say, well, here's the thought behind it, and here's what the therapist told me. I also had a therapist read every script.

That would be my next question.

That was something I brought in, in Year Two. So at least I could always explain why his character would say something. Sometimes there's a mistake. Or there's different ways to go. Sometimes I would watch Gabriel and I would see he was getting more emotionally involved and sometimes he would be kind of clinical. There was a big scene with Allison Peale where he basically forces her to go to chemo and he even takes her there, it was the climax of their relationship. And it had been written articulately but clinically and when they rehearsed it, Gabriel was no longer a psychiatrist with a patient, he was a father with his daughter, and that was much more interesting dramatically. And that was always subtextually there but – he wanted to go on his feet, he wanted to drop all masks, so I rewrote that scene in the direction I saw him pushing. The writer at that moment got very upset with me, I was changing her script. It ended up being the writer's favorite episode; it was just that in that moment she was not able to make a 180-degree change. You just have to hope you are making the right choice, because if you're wrong the writer will never forgive you. And even if you're right the writer will remember how angry he or she was with you. But Gabriel's gut was correct there. Get the words out of the way. Don't give them paragraphs, give them six words to say and let them push the scene.

Lights Out *was more traditional in the way you run the room, is that right?*

Yes, that was a real writers' room experience. On *In Treatment* there were not even staff writers. There were freelance writers. I stopped having a room once production started. They'd come in, they'd drop off their episodes. Halfway through I asked for another week of the room, just to catch up on everyone. *Lights Out*[3] was different in many ways. There I took over a busted pilot. The pilot had been shot, and it had not worked except that the star, an unknown actor, was terrific. And there were certain elements they liked, and they wanted a rewrite. They didn't want to reshoot the whole pilot, they wanted me to keep as much as I could and back in another story into the pilot and recontextualize some of the scenes they had. It was technically the most tricky job I'd ever done. It would have been easier to start from scratch. But they'd already spent six or seven million dollars and they didn't want to throw that out, they didn't want to admit they needed to throw that out. They had spent 15 days shooting the pilot, and we ended up reshooting for another seven days and the seven days became 75% of the pilot. There was no sense of where the series would go from the original pilot – which was the other reason I was brought in. So I ended up rewriting the pilot and writing an episode too, and they said OK, we'll go to series. And then I put a room together and that was a traditional writers' room.

How many writers?

Small. One staffer, four writers and me. We started out with really just the four; the staffer didn't even join us till we were in production.

Actually that's a handy size, five people. Let everyone get a chance to speak, more than that can get into too many different directions. So we had four writer-producers and one staffer. The staffer is just a WGA designation, where you get a set rate. But I had writer-producers because I needed writers who can go to the set. And then actually as the season went on, we had a couple of freelancers. I imagine five years ago I would have had twice the staff.

So writers' rooms are getting smaller?

Sure. These writers were paid by the studio, but we worked here in this office. Every writer had a desk but they didn't have a walled office. Some writers like it a lot and it creates a community in a sense, and some writers kind of want to wall off and they have a hard time adjusting. The stages are usually in miserable places in New York. So our stage was at the foot of the Triborough Bridge in Queens, too hard to get to and nobody wants to go there unless they have to, when shooting starts. And this place is quieter and less crazy.

Do you think that the tradition of writers' rooms is why American TV writing is so successful?

Actually, that was the first legitimate room I've been in. And the first thing I did was I read through the two episodes I had written myself, and they were cruel to me. They were much more critical to me than I would ever be to them. It's always easier to be critical than to actually have to do it. Just because I was a showrunner didn't mean I was impervious to ego harm. But the room is smarter than the individual. It's a bigger brain. You just need one guy saying, No, I hear what you're saying but that's too soon, if we do that in Episode Two we have no place to go. You need people who are really smart and bring slightly different things to it and you can't have too strong an ego yourself and you cannot have writers in there for whom winning is more important. There's a certain kind of alpha male personality that can destroy a writers' room. Somebody who doesn't get it and they keep going and keep going – that guy can ruin the room. So it's a lot about chemistry. You need one guy who's a little off and most of what he says you'll go, What? But then, once in a while he'll say something that nobody else will think of.

How do you put a room together?

This was a show about boxing, so one guy had been a serious high school boxer, another guy was an MMA fighter who was in sports but I also had two guys who between them knew every fight that had taken place in the last 30 years. So they would mention a fight, and we would go on YouTube, and watch it. I had one writer from the *Mad Men* writers' room. I had one writer who has three daughters, I have two daughters, the woman writer had sisters. I don't want a show with three daughters and have an all male staff or nobody with daughters, you want a bit of a mix, you want a cultural mix to a degree.

Now that you say cultural mix, it does look like American TV is mostly written by white men.

You got a lot of white men, yeah. So there's that problem. If it's an all-Jewish writing room and my lead character is an Irish Catholic boxer that's not good. A big part of the show was about the boxer's marriage so it was helpful to me to have a writer who has been in a long complicated relationship. If you can't get a cultural mix, and there's various reasons it's difficult to do that, you're in trouble. Class mix is helpful too; what I don't want is five spoilt Beverly Hills guys writing a spoof on boxing. I need self-made writers. I am mostly writing blue collar characters and it turns out self-made writers who worked their way up have done better work for me than people who have been sort of handed everything. One of my tests when a writer comes in for a meeting with me the first time, and they usually have coffee or milk, is, do they take their dirty dish with them when they leave? If you leave your dirty stuff behind it just means you're used to having someone cleaning up after you. You're not gonna pitch in. And if an episode is shooting tomorrow and things don't work, and you're not the writer of that episode but I ask you to do me a favor and rewrite the daughter scene, will you do it? Everyone is pitching in on everyone's episode and credit has nothing to do with it. There's no relationship between who writes what and how credit is determined in TV, it's a very bad credit system we have. So we will distribute credit evenly. I will try to reward the people who work harder with a little more credit as the season goes on. But there are people who only care about credit and that kills you.

This also relates to the money you get within that system, right?

It's related to the money and it's related to your next job. I think the L.A. writers are much more hierarchical and there's a lot more sense of, I want to get to the next level. Most people in New York probably don't know what the different titles mean. But everyone in L.A. knows the difference between a supervising producer and a co-producer. You wanna move up that ladder in Los Angeles. In New York there's not that many rooms and you're happy to be on a show in New York so it works differently.

How many drafts does a writer get before you step in?

It depends. At the end of the season everyone's working three times faster. So you have like four days to get me a draft, maybe I have to take it from you and do an allnighter and we start prepping it the next day. We had a couple of episodes at the end where I had two allnighters on the draft. And that's a killer. Because you're working an 80-hour week and then you throw in another allnighter, to get the rewrite done. Some of the writers reach a point where they can't do any more, people get sick, people have family problems – and ultimately it's your job as a showrunner to get it right. So we beat out in the room, the first draft in broad strokes and then I say, you're gonna write this episode and so you put the cards on the board and we all work the storyline. But if you know you have to write that episode you're gonna be much more engaged in getting that work and then we go on to the next episode and I assign the writers to each of them. By Episode Seven everybody had gone once, cause I did the first two, and we were losing one staffer so it was time to regroup. But the problem is once you're done with seven episodes one of your writers is unavailable to plot because he's on the set shooting, another writer is unavailable to plot because he's prepping his episode, he's going on location, another writer is unavailable to plot because he's trying to get his episode ready to publish that week, so your writers' room – there is no writers' room at a certain point in the season. So by the second go-round on that show I basically turn in to plot it individually with each writer and if someone can come in to the room that day that's great. But it gets lonelier as the season gets on.

So what is the difference between being a showrunner and just being a writer? Do you get less time to write?

Well, I get less time for writing, but I edit. It can take somewhere between four hours and 60 hours on one episode. And that's really the final rewrite. Every edit is mine. I rewrite every episode as well, I always do the final pass on every episode, sometimes I rewrite, a showrunner can rewrite from 100% of an episode to 10% of an episode. It depends on what I got, how the draft came in, how burned out the writer is, what kind of time pressure I'm on.

Do you actually change writers during the season when that happens?

Yes. My assistant had been in the room whenever it was plotted out, so he helped on one episode. I had a script supervisor-coordinator, the guy who gets everything right, I threw him a teleplay. The producing writers are contracted for the season so if someone is not working out you need to let them go and pay them off their entire salary, or you keep them on staff and hope they can recover or they can do something for you. And sometimes they can and sometimes they can't. But on other shows ... on *Criminal Intent*, for instance, I had a little money kind of tucked away in the budget. If everything was falling apart, I could bring in one more writer for the last two or three episodes. The problem is then I've now worked on eight drafts of nine episodes, and I've edited six of them, so you bring someone new to help you out and how do you get her up to speed. By the time you've explained where the show is you could have done it yourself.

That's the question always: why don't you do it yourself?

Because I have to go to the set, I have to cast, I have notes from the studio, I have notes from the network ...

What about that? How great is your creative control toward the studio and the network?

You know, it was interesting. FX[4] reads every word of every draft really carefully. I've done NBC, HBO and FX. On *In Treatment* it was almost impossible for the studio and the network to keep up with notes because we were turning out 30 pages every day. There was an executive producer, sometimes he would give notes on something. I will always listen to notes and I will always have the conversations and I hope to get to a point in the season where they realize ... I don't pretend to listen, I listen trying to understand their problem, you know. This is bothering you, well, here's why we're doing it. If you're working with rational, thoughtful people and have rational, thoughtful discussions, then it's good. Sometimes an outsider brings up something that you thought was clear, and you realize while you're talking to them that they have no idea that there's a romance growing between these two characters, that they missed it entirely – and that's good to know. I found the FX people were extremely literate; there were maybe three strong disagreements in the course of the season and most of the time their notes were surprisingly helpful or reminded me of something that needed clarification. But there were a couple just flat out disagreements that I had, and at a certain point midway through the season, I'd say, look, you must know by now I take your notes seriously, so if I say "no" five times, I probably mean no. So either tell me I have to make the change anyway or just stop asking me. Otherwise figure I am being respectful but I don't want to do it.

Where do you think the changes come from? Are they dramaturgical or is there some kind of other agenda?

Every company is different. At the network they're making sure your leads are likeable. They're protecting the leads – and that can make for bland TV at times. FX likes complicated, flawed characters. Sometimes it comes from anecdotal observations somebody in their staff has had, so I have to explain, no, this is where it's heading, so they need clarification. Sometimes it's a concern that it's something they've seen before, it's familiar. Some of the notes are production notes, like we possibly cannot shoot that in seven days. These I take very seriously.

Will you hear things like "The audience won't like that"?

Nobody knows what the audience will like. But sometimes they'll say it, yes. One of the things apparently, even on *Mad Men* – apparently that writers' room wanted the wife to have an affair at some point. And the rule on TV is "the wife can't cheat" (laugh). So they ended up with her cheating but she didn't like it or it was just to get back at him and it was a mistake.

This is hilarious.

The wife cannot cheat on American TV.

So there are ethical rules.

Well, there are, but you don't know what they are until you violate them. Apparently the audience will put up with a lot of character flaw in its male leads, and much less character flaw in its female leads. I think *Nurse Jackie* is interesting because it's pushing that limit – but that's an unusual show. And the actress is inherently likeable so she can get away with things a character couldn't get away with. Anyway. It's one of those unwritten laws.

Where do you think it comes from?

I suspect that they've learned over time that the audience will turn off on the wife. You will lose sympathy for the wife if she does this. Some of these rules may have no basis on fact. There are a lot of shows that say, we don't wanna see poor people robbing or killing poor people, the audience isn't interested in that. There are certain things that people have decided over time. If you look at network television, I don't think there are many strictly black shows any more.

That's true.

And so it's very tough if you watch *NCIS* or *CSI*, there suddenly you see black on black crime, which is by the way the most common crime in America. You will not see that on American television anymore – the victims on a lot of crime shows are generally speaking wealthy people, the murderers are very wealthy. *Southland* is an exception but most TV crime is high end. 'Cause nobody really believes the audience wants to see the crimes of the ghetto.

And that's where you get a misrepresentation.

Yeah. But when you try it out, if the ratings drop within three episodes of when you did it, they say, see?

Do you feel there is enough space for you to try out things?

Well, on *Criminal Intent* once or twice a year I would do a show like that and I would endure a certain amount of criticism from Dick Wolf. I think one of the best episodes we did was based on a senseless triple murder in New York. Some immigrant kids killed some black kids who were home for the holidays from college, having escaped from that neighborhood, and they were killed for no reason at all, that was a heartbreak of an episode. I'm pretty sure the episode did not lose us viewers, but I got a lot of lectures about "Don't do too many of those", you know. (laugh) Another one is: if it's a cop show they don't wanna see a lot of corrupt cops. Possibly because the cop shows are in good relations with the cops because they shoot there. Old school believes that your characters must be heroic, so network wants the cops to be heroes, not to make mistakes. In cable it's different; *The Wire* was not like that, *The Shield* was not like that.

Do you think cable is getting more and more conservative though?

Well, here's what's happening with cable: it's too competitive now. Like I have a very good show about a boxer and it's up against a show called *The Game* about NFL football players and their girl-friends, it's up against *Southland*, it's up against *Teen Mom*. It used to be different. If you had a scripted drama on cable you were the only scripted drama that night on that slot and everybody managed. You know, Sunday night was HBO, Saturday night was FX, but now, there's a lot of competition. There's network brands now, so each net-work has a certain type of show that they know they can promote, that their audience knows they can find when they tune in. I don't know if it makes it more conservative, but there's more of a sameness within each network. I'd still say the most challenging, character-driven shows are cable shows. *Nurse Jackie* could not be a network show. *Lights Out* could not be a network show. *Southland* failed as a network show. There are shows which would not last an hour on network. And there are shows on cable that are sort of summer network shows.

Grey's Anatomy *had a cheating wife, by the way.*

Oh yeah. That's an ensemble show, there you may be able to afford it. But seriously, *Mad Men* had an enormous discussion about it. And *Mad Men* is on cable and it's meant to be a barrier-breaking show, and Matt (Weiner) comes out of the David Chase writers' room and still... You know, it's like with any one of these beliefs. People don't question them, they hold them very dearly.

Doesn't it also depend on your pull as a showrunner?

I think a lot of showrunners, even the ones that we know are the most rule-breaking, tough guys, they have internalized certain rules. To be honest, I don't think the pressure to not have Janet cheat would come from AMC. I think that was Matt who was probably nervous about it. And that's probably where a room with people who don't look like you is good. If there's inspiring women writers in the room, when that comes up, you know, it will be a different argument. And people, writers have a cultural perspective to their work that they are not always aware of. So you know, I need someone in the room to stick up for the 15 year old daughter because she was once a 15 year old girl – it's probably easier for her to do that than for me. It's easier to have someone saying, Oh no, I hated my parents when they were doing that.

That's fascinating that you do that through the constellation of the writers' room.

I try to almost cast the room.

So you actually look at people's biographies. I mean, beyond their work and their filmographies.

I try to read what they are writing. And most of the time people write organically, they're writing about themselves and their lives one way or another, in everything they do. So I want to know what themes are interesting to you and I want to make sure I cast you correctly.

Is TV satisfying to you as a playwright?

Lights Out was thrilling to write and I felt like I was doing some of the best writing in my career. It was thrilling to plot a longer form. A play or a screenplay is a one-off. And this was 13 episodes. It may end up being only 13 but that's already a nice long arc.

So did you think of the season as one screenplay?

Yes. We had a three-act structure for the season. And we were very aware that we were building towards the climax of his comeback. The first four episodes were Act One, at the end of fourth episode it's clear there's no end to the drama, that they aren't accepting him to go back to the ring. Episodes Five through Nine were Act Two, the middle of the season, which is page 60 of a screenplay in my mind. It was the first comeback fight, and the last episodes lead to the big rematch. And there was the pilot, and each of the 12 episodes was supposed to be around a fight. He's going up against his family, he's going up against his family of origin, he's going up against the fight promoter. There was a cinematic structure to the season.

This doesn't happen very often in TV.

No. And I'm not sure you can always pull it off. I'm not even sure I could do it with the second season of the show because it does not have an overriding mission like this one. I think that three-act structure is a valuable thing to have, even within a scene. I think you should always have a three-act structure. And certainly a season should have a sense of where a character is on his journey. And if you swing in halfway across the lake, you're too exhausted to go to the other side and it's too late to go back – that's always to me the midpoint. The midpoint is the fight he has against an opponent he should not be anywhere near. I just had that great arc going for me in this, and in some ways I felt like I was writing the whole thing – I actually wrote the pilot, the second episode and the finale, these are my teleplays and I obviously contributed to others. So you're opening the story and you're ending the story. I wanted to write the finale, and I wrote it in one night when I had to, I was just waiting to get to it.

Do you like switching forms, you know, TV, theater, the movies?

I do, but theater is glacial in the time it takes to get something produced. And movies most of the time means screenplays that don't get made. There is a joy in TV – I have more control of my storyline here, in some ways more than as a playwright. And it's hard to get a play made, it's just hard to get them up nowadays. While in four months I did 35 episodes of *In Treatment*, in four months at *Lights Out* we did 13 episodes, that's an awful lot of storytelling. You are lucky to get a play every three years in New York, you know, and the wait drives me crazy. I like being under that kind of gun.

So what comes after Lights Out?

I don't know. That's the other thing about TV. We killed ourselves on *Lights Out* and I think it's partly the best year of television I've done and the reviews were better than anything I've done since *Side Man* that won the Tony.[5] But TV reviews don't matter so much. We're in a bad time slot, we're fighting for our life. It's a little like theater. It's a roll of the dice every single time. You get used to that from theater, you know. You can have a play that everyone loves. And if the New York Times gives you a bad review, it's closing, or you can get a good review and still not do box office, 'cause you don't have a name actor. So you're always aware of how short your life can be in theater, and in TV it's the same. In TV pretty much every spring you're wondering what's your next job, will you have to start another show from scratch? That's an awful lot of work. Year One of *Lights Out* was much harder than Year Six of *Criminal Intent*, my second year as a showrunner and the sixth year as a show. I could have died and probably there would be seven shows out before anyone noticed. The crew knows what they're doing, you're not bringing in crew, you're not teaching the editors, the directors have been with you for a number of years, there's a shorthand, you're not reinventing the wheel. The first year of a TV show is an enormous lift.

Especially if it's original material.

Actors are figuring out where their characters are, the DP [Director of Photography] is figuring out how to shoot the thing and how to light it and how much time we have.

But it's fascinating as well.

Yeah, but it's all-consuming. *Lights Out* was a seven-day shoot and that was a whole different schedule than an eight-day shoot and I didn't realize how much more complicated that was. Not just that it makes it harder to make your day production-wise but pre-production is shorter. And you need that extra weekend. When you're eight days, you get that extra weekend almost every time; when you're seven days, you don't, you only have one weekend. Just the logistics of it are tough. I realized we couldn't do company moves, we had to leave the show on location, because the travel time would kill us, we couldn't afford it.

So do you always have projects that are ready to go?

No. I wrote a pilot this winter, but it doesn't look like it's getting picked up. And now I am at a crossroads. I'm waiting to hear about *Lights Out*, I'm getting offers. If *Lights Out* doesn't go, I'm trying to think what I want to do. Second year of this show, tenth year of that show – I don't know what I'm in the mood for at the moment. And to not be going 90 hours a week is unusual.

What does that feel like?

It's disorientating.

But you need some free time too.

Yeah, I haven't had this in the last four years. One show would end and the next thing would go right away, and I had to jump on it. *In Treatment* ended at an awkward time of the year and I was lucky that *Lights Out* presented itself when it did – but it meant that instead of taking the summer off I was busy in August, desperately trying to get the show going. If I were only doing network TV there would be a sort of a natural season to it – because I've gone from network to cable to off calendar cable it's just trickier. And it's easier for me to be in sixth year than, like, second. I can go non-stop, but it's true, I wouldn't mind slowing it down for a while.

Is that even possible or is there always an anxiety that you kind of lose momentum?

Oh yeah, if I don't grab something by May, then I can be out of work for a year.

Is it that bad?

(laughs) Yeah.

Why?

Well, I think you always want to have some income. And it's a weird muscle to keep up, it's very hard to start it again from scratch. There's a lot of writers who will take that year and write their own play, but I've always been a deadline writer and I thrive under that – I just know that about myself at this point. I need to know someone is waiting for it and that it's gonna be made.

Don't you burn out, or have writer's block?

I have writer's block when there's no deadline. I have as much block as I can afford within the structure of having to shoot it on Monday. (laugh) You really can't have writer's block when you're shooting it on Monday and it's Friday night. You just keep writing till it's finished.

Do you enjoy the production side? You sound like you do.

Yes. I like working with the actors enormously.

And that's something you learned by doing?

The actors I learned to work with in theater. Theater taught me a lot about who to cast, what their process is, that's a big help for me. I think a lot of showrunners have only written in rooms, but I like working with the designers, they're usually so sharp and they're very literate, and it just gets better and better. If you have those guys in the right spots, I mean, even the production manager guys. A lot of times there's a creative solution to what seems to be an annoying budget problem. We had a scene in *Lights Out*, we wanted the teaser to take place in an aquarium, that's in Coney Island. But once we're out there, we're in the middle of nowhere and we can't afford to drive out to shoot one scene for two hours – and we also had a scene with his major opponent, there's gonna be some sort of getting to know your scene. So we decided his opponent has something going in the projects. It was a walk and talk scene, it made perfect sense for his character and that was a very clever solution. In that case I let production drive the decision. It was consistent with the character that he grew up there. And it was a rollercoaster and it worked really well, and that's fun for me.

What about directing?

I directed one movie, and I directed one episode of *In Treatment*. You're doing a lot of directing as a showrunner, you're on the set. The directors are terrific but they don't know the story and the characters and the actors as well. So by the time you get to the set you've gone over with each actor what the episode's about in as much detail as is needed and then you're on the set and you go over the key scenes – you're doing a lot of directing in another way. The actors' arc is my responsibility, not the director's on the set. I know where the character's going, I know where the character's been, while the director is there for a certain amount of days and then he goes on to the next one. And if they come in for Episode Eight, they're good guys and they watched all seven that came before, but still – that character's arc is my responsibility.

And you choose the directors, right?

And by now I know so many. I had this guy from *Criminal Intent* and I brought him in for the reshoots of *Lights Out*, and he directed three more. We're perfect together, those are nice collaborations. If I'd stop to direct an episode, then the next episode isn't going to be ready, and the one after that isn't going to be plotted so the only one you can really direct is the last episode of the season, and the last episode of the season was a flat out boxing match with the crowds and it was well beyond my directorial abilities. I can direct actors decently, I can stage a few people in the room adequately, I can block the camera, but TV is technically very demanding. I think almost everyone can direct their own feature 'cause even on a low budget film you have 28 days, which is four times the shooting for half as much paper. But technically to direct these 45-page episodes in seven days is a very demanding task, so I defer to their technical expertise and they defer to my knowledge of the characters and it works out pretty well.

Is that normal, seven days for 45 pages?

Network is eight, some cable is seven, HBO is a hundred. (laughs) Yes, seven is the norm now in a lot of basic cable. And it's tough. The pressure it puts on … First day of pre-production, you have a production meeting, somewhere in there you also need cast, somewhere in there you also need to find locations, you have to have a cast read-through, you have to have a meeting the day before production begins, you want a tone meeting with the director, you have to educate him on the script, that can take hours. So how are you supposed to be doing all that in pre-production? If that's four days' worth of work in pre-production I'd rather have those four days out of eight than four out of seven and that's when it starts to gang up on you.

Amazing. And still, there's a lot of series which look like cinema.

Our show is gorgeous. I brought in a DP from independent film, and he's an artist, we got a really good look for seven days. I had almost no wasted scenes. I don't think we deleted five scenes the whole season. I had to write much more economically, and I just decided to not shoot something we're not gonna use. The risk is you have a scene that you don't like which you have to use because there's nothing else, but you know, on *Criminal Intent* we would publish 58-page scripts, and every rough cut would come in at 15 minutes longer and then the edit was brutal. It's murderous when you cut out the red herrings because they didn't pay off, that's stupid. So in this show the rough cuts would come in at 45, 46 minutes usually and the cut was 41 minutes, mostly you're taking air out.

Did you use less dialogue?

It depends. The editors will say, why don't we just lose all this blablabla. They don't wanna say it to the writer; the editors in general don't want the writer in the room. They want to know that when you come into the edit room you're looking at everything fresh, it doesn't matter what you wrote, it doesn't matter what you shot, now you have to find the best story. Writers kill themselves to get the film to where they wanted it to go and they have a hard time just letting go. Even if something doesn't work, they'll get mad if it doesn't work, they will see that it doesn't work and still... The answer is yes, they'll say, you probably don't need it. But I love that scene.

It depends on where the writer comes from, right?

Absolutely. I think that playwrights cling more. But that's something you have to learn and most of the time writers don't get into the edit room, it's the showrunner's job or the producer's job. When you shot a movie you got two weeks off and the editor assembles the cut in the meantime, so when you come back in, you had a little distance on it, there was time. TV is such a fast process that learning to let go immediately is important. The rewrites: I get a draft, the writer's dead, I need a rewrite in a day, and I'm like, chop this, get rid of that. Some writers can't make that transition quickly enough – and then it's time to edit and it's just hard. That's the advantage of a showrunner in the edit room. I didn't usually initiate the episode, or I learned to be brutal, to me the edit was another writing pass. And I love those collaborations with the editors. But almost every editor I've ever worked with, if I say, listen, I can't get to the edit room, do you want me to send in the writer? They'll say no. (laughs)

And in the movies they don't want the writer on set either.

But that comes from a power structure. In TV no director thinks he's the auteur. It's a much more collaborative environment. And I always have my writers on set when we shoot. I think it's important because they know best what the original intentions were. Ideally they also know when to pull the brake. If it's 14 hours in and it doesn't work, it's time to let it go. That's something the writers have to learn, just being there and knowing when to say something. You know, on *Law and Order*, before I took over the show, the writers were not supposed to be on set. Dick doesn't want the writers interfering with production and he doesn't want production interfering with editing.

Although he's a writer himself.

(laughs) It's a weird set of skills you need to have as a showrunner. And a lot of writers cannot be a showrunner, that's the vast majority.

TV writing now reminds me sometimes of the movies of the 70s.

Yeah, yeah. And they stopped making these movies. I look at those movies and I think, how would that get sold today? How would that even get pitched? It couldn't happen. *Fat City*, the John Huston boxing movie, you know, with Stacey Keach as the boxer? He's the dad in our TV show. I went and looked at *Fat City* when this job came on, that's how I thought of Stacey. But there's no way anyone would make that movie now. It's, like, the spiritual path of the defeated. Well, that's a terrible pitch. Movies have become, not all but too many of them, big and it takes a lot to promote them, so they need blockbusters, sequels, it's become a different kind of business and the independent film has fewer and fewer theaters. So TV, and I don't think I'm saying that because I'm doing TV now, I think TV is at the moment the best place for a writer to be. There's virtually no way to make a living in theater, and there's no interest in a stray play unless you cast usually inappropriate superstars in your stray play. And movies...I just think the big corporate companies, they're like ocean liners, they're big enterprises, they can't move too quickly. Independent movies, you spend all your time trying to get them made, a little cable show, you do 13 episodes, two and a half million dollars apiece. No one's gonna lose their shirt on that, there's enough places to sell it overseas and there's enough rerun afterlife eventually, and DVD sales I suppose, eventually it will work itself out. And people have come to expect more challenging stuff on cable. Maybe I don't wanna spend 100 dollars to go to a movie with my wife and get a sitter, but if I can turn on AMC and see an episode of *Breaking Bad*, that's pretty good. It's interesting how it shifted. Nobody would have predicted 20 years ago that TV would be where it is now.

But don't you sometimes have a story which you would like to see turned into a movie?

I like writing screenplays but more often than not they didn't get made or if they did get made I was humiliated by the process.

You mean by the director.

It is the director and it is the miscasting, there's too much of that. I'll never have that power unless I write and direct my own movie. But, you know, it took me three years to get the movie that I wrote and directed, I was ten hours of the day on the phone. On TV you may have pressure that can debilitate you but on the other hand I'll make 13 episodes in four months. And you learn so much more writing and editing an episode and then writing and editing another, you learn so much in that process, more than writing your own screenplay and waiting for it to get made. You know, where I am now as a writer to where I was four years ago before I began showrunning – it's probably close to 90 episodes in four years.

That's a lot.

Exactly. And there's a moment where you know what you're doing and then you can improvise. Things are under my fingers now.

That's an excellent point you're making here. What about TV movies?

That's gone. Lifetime does the sort of raped-by-a-serial-killer movie of the month. But that genre's gone. Cable series for the moment is a pretty good thing, even if the budgets are cut and the staffs are cut. It's the most expressive writing you can do and make a living for now. I miss my movies and I think about pitching them and I think about going out there and trying to hook up with a director. But I hate wasting time waiting for something to get a green light, that's not time you get back.

Thank you so much, and if I do have something else I want to ask...

Just make up an answer for me.

Tom Fontana

Tom Fontana has written and produced *St. Elsewhere, Homicide: Life on the Street, Oz* and *The Philanthropist*. Currently, he is filming *Borgia* (Canal+ and Netflix) and *Copper* (BBC America). He has received, among others, three Emmy awards, four Peabody awards, three Writers' Guild awards, four Television Critics Association awards, the Cable Ace award, the Humanitas Prize, a Special Edgar and the first prize at the Cinema Tout Ecran Festival in Geneva.

So how did you get to writing for TV? And stay in New York while doing that?

(laughs) I was born in New York, in Buffalo, to a very non-showbiz family. And I started writing when I was very very young. My parents took us to see a production of *Alice in Wonderland* and I went home and started writing dialogue although I had no idea what it was, and I just kept writing. I was writing in high school and I was writing in college, writing plays, then I moved to New York. I was having a play done up at the Williamstown Theater Festival in Massachusetts. Then, that summer, Bruce Paltrow came, who was the husband of Blythe Danner and has since passed away. Blythe was an actress in one of the companies, there were two of them. My play was done in the Second Company. Blythe brought their two children to the play, Gwyneth and Jake Paltrow (both very young at the time). They loved the play and they kept saying to Bruce, "You have to come and see this." Bruce was a big TV producer and I was a playwright, I don't like TV. (laughs) So the whole summer went by and Bruce never saw the play and Blythe was mad at him for that. He was just starting to do this show *St. Elsewhere*, and she kind of forced him to hire me for an episode. And I'm convinced to this day that if he had seen the play he would never have hired me. So my whole career is based on having no ambition whatsoever and having good luck and a very sweet guardian angel named Blythe Danner.

This is a beautiful thing you said right there. You know, I keep hearing two names in New York. The one is Bruce Paltrow's and the other is your name. And they all say the same things about you both, they say you are like Bruce.

Well, he was my mentor, he was my rabbi, he was ... you know.

Bruce Paltrow seems to be that legend of a mentor, always bringing people very generously together or into the business. And you are known for the same generosity. You are a renowned and powerful TV writer now, but the first thing people tell me every time your name is mentioned, is how very generous you are. Aren't competitiveness and nondisclosure the mantra of this industry? Why and how are you different?

Actually I said this to Bruce once. "Bruce, what am I going to do, how can I ever repay you?" He said, "Well, the truth is, Tom, you can't ever repay me. There's never gonna be a time when you can do for me what I have done for you. But there will be a time where you can do it for somebody else. So do it for somebody else and you'll have paid me back."

What an amazing fellow.

Yes. I took that to heart. Listen, our business is indeed very competitive but I don't need to be successful over the bodies of other people. If I'm going to be successful I just want to be successful because what I do has value, I don't want to be successful because I've crashed someone else's career, I don't think I'd enjoy the success knowing I'd gotten it that way.

And you are so successful, that the European broadcasters came looking for you. You are probably the first American writer running a TV show financed completely by the European market. And you are dealing with European commissioning editors, who are used to working with writers who are much less spoilt than you. I mean the European TV writer, although he is better off than in the cinema, is far from having the power and creative freedom of an American TV writer. How was it working in such an environment, after being used to calling the shots?

(laughs) To be absolutely honest, I am enjoying the experience tremendously not having to deal with an American studio.

Is that so?

Well, in the same way as a European writer is used to the trials and tribulations of dealing with a European network, I'm so used to the slings and arrows of dealing with American studios. It's a different experience, obviously, but you still get frustrated. I've had two other great creative freedom experiences. One was working at MTM with Bruce. The company doesn't exist anymore, but back then it was a very writer-driven company. The second time was when I did *Oz* for HBO. The amount of creative freedom and encouragement they gave me was extraordinary.

It's not TV, it's HBO.

Exactly. It was Chris Albrecht and Anne Thomopoulos. There was a great sense of "We hired you because you know how to do this and we're gonna leave you alone." And that's the way I feel here. It's not that executives shouldn't have opinions, but at HBO and Lagardère there's very much a sense of "We're gonna give you our opinion and then you're gonna make a decision, because you're the one with the vision about what this series should look like and thematically cover."

So they treat you like a director. Because in Europe only directors get the treatment you describe. How did you manage to make them treat you like a director?

Yeah, they're looking at the American showrunner model, and they're seeing finally that maybe giving the writer at least some power is gonna give them a better television program. And that is the Catch-22 of the showrunner deal: all writers want total creative freedom. But coming with that, has to be the financial responsibility of how the show is made. So, you can't be a showrunner and say, "I don't care what it costs," because then you're not a showrunner, you're not a writer-producer, you're simply a writer. And if we wanna get European writers empowered, there has to be a change in the attitude of the writer as well. It's not just a change in the attitude of the studio or the network. You know what I mean?

So how can a writer get trained to be a producer?

I was not a producer. Bruce Paltrow taught me how to be a producer. He taught me how to write for television, and he taught me how to produce for television. And he was very clear to me that I had a moral responsibility to protect the financial investment, that it wasn't my money but I had to treat it as if it was my money. And that's what I teach when I bring in young writers and move them up through the chain of command. It's one of the big lessons. It's a very difficult lesson. I know how to make a series work.

Without compromising on the quality.

Exactly. Where you say, "I have this set and I wrote this scene for that set, but rather than building a whole new set, can I actually put this scene on that other set and still have it be a viable scene?" I happen to believe that a good scene will play anywhere. So I can put you and me in this room or I can put us in a street corner in Prague in a rain storm – the heart of the scene will be the same, regardless of the environment. Unless you're doing a mass, then you have to be in a church.

It is still hard to believe that the European broadcasters gave you full control.

Well, I would not have taken the job if I was going to be in the position of a European writer. Because I understand what a weak position that is. So the whole idea was if you want an American showrunner then you have to play by conventional rules. And it's been an adjustment. But I feel very good about the collaboration. It wasn't easy, it's easy now.

What would you say is the main difference?

The hardest thing for me was not in terms of the writing, there they have been wonderfully open. It's the producing side. I know crews in New York. I know who the best carpenter is. I know who the best grip is. I know who the best prop person is. I don't know anybody in Europe. And not only don't I know anybody, I don't even know if the functions are the same as they are in America. So for me these past months were an education. I should say, we have 18 different countries between the actors and the crew. This is the way it's done there, so I've had to adjust their mindset and my mindset to make it work better. But I also had to acknowledge that sometimes that's the way things are, good or bad. I've had to learn how to accommodate the things I could not change. There's a different dynamic on a New York sound stage than there is on a Czech stage. Not better, just different.

Do you think the series would have been different if you did it here?

Well, from a location point of view we couldn't have done it here. There's nothing that looks like it. Other than that, because things seem to take longer in Prague than I've experienced here in America, we would have had more coverage and we would have been able to spend more time on each scene. But again, it's taken me all this time to figure out why shooting goes as slowly as it does. Is it just this particular circumstance and all the other crews normally move faster or is it just that it's a kind of New York thing, "let's shoot it quickly," and in Prague there isn't that imperative? There is an American but certainly a New York kind of energy and aggressiveness about shooting that everybody in Prague, perfectly wonderful and talented, doesn't have. They just don't seem to be in a hurry. (laughs)

And what about the writing? Would the scripts have been different, if you had been working with an American network?

Like I said Canal+ and ZDF were very unintrusive. We had a lot of conversations before I started writing – about what the show could be thematically and visually, how much sex there should be, and how much violence.

How much?

Well, the French wanted more sex and the Germans want less. (laughs) And I think partially because in Germany we're gonna be on free TV, while Canal+, the French network, is Pay TV. So Canal+ is much more like HBO, and ZDF feels more like a broadcast television network here. We're literally making two versions of the show, but they're not different in terms of character or theme. It's just that on one you're gonna see penises and vaginas and on the other you won't.

That's a quirky idea, doing a show for HBO and ABC at the same time . . . So you were never told that the characters should be more sympathetic?

No.

You sure you worked in Europe?

(laughs)

Did you have a writers' room?

Well, I never do a writers' room writers' room. We get together but not in a "let's sit around and write stories" way. In most writers' rooms, everyone comes in at nine o' clock to break stories, but out of eight hours, you spend at least an hour and a half eating, you spend at least two hours talking about your life, an hour on your cell, and so the actual amount of time that the necessary work gets done, is a relatively small part of a very long day. What works for me is I sit down one on one with the writer who's gonna write that episode. Normally what I do, and I do it with *Borgia* too, I write a bible for all 12 episodes. And I say, "Here are some potential scenes for this episode." And once I've done the bible everybody reads it and we sit down and talk, but it's a reaction to what I've done as opposed to "let's all sit in a room and begin the process." I think that one person has to be responsible for the vision of the show and you invite the other writers to help shape it, fill it out. What I love about the writers who I work with is, they're always coming up with stuff that I never would have thought of. But all the ideas come off an outline that I've written.

So you do discuss the outline.

Yes, and the outline becomes as useless a document as it could possibly be.

So how detailed is that outline?

It's detailed in enumerating a series of incidents. "This is the incident of this moment." But my whole thing is, I don't say, "this is what I want," because if you say to another writer "this is what I want," that's what you get, and I don't want to be handed back scenes which I could write myself. I want someone giving me something where I can go, "Holy shit, I never thought of that, that is such a great approach to the scene, that dialogue there is just so fucking good, it blows my mind." And that's why the whole room full of writers thing seems kind of reductive to me.

So you don't think that that's the secret of success of American TV?

No. I have writers here, they have offices, they run up and down the hallway, exchanging ideas, working shit out, sharing.

But they all have their own rooms.

They all have their own rooms, exactly! And if somebody has a problem, they come to me or they go to one of the other writers. It's more of a writers' community, we're not stuck in this room for eight hours.

So you get the first draft back and do you then do a rewrite?

What I always say to the writer is, "With the first draft you teach me how to write this show. With the second draft I'll teach you how to write this show." So I want them to feel totally free to try anything they want. And when I get the script, I'm not judgmental, what I say is, "Think about this, think about that." Because the other mistake some showrunners make is, they tell another writer how they would have written the script. I think that's wrong. Then I give the writer notes, I say, "This wasn't as clear, I don't really understand her journey, How did she get to this point?" I ask questions and sometimes I have suggestions, but I'm never dogmatic about my suggestions. Once the second draft is done and I have to get it ready for production, I have to roll up my sleeves and do whatever I need to do, whether it is fixing something that the other writer didn't get or didn't get to, or which the production demands. So I have to come up with a solution to any problems. The first drafts of all of the *Borgia* episodes were probably 75 pages long. When we got to production they had to get down to 50 pages.

How long is your slot?

It's somewhere between 48 and 52. So, here I had to now take someone else's script and take 25 pages out. You know as well as I do you take this scene out and you got to fix that scene or take another scene out. I try not to throw out anything, I try to keep as much of the original writer's material as possible. Sometimes freelance writers will call me and they'll go, "You know I wrote that phrase for this scene and suddenly it was over there in that other scene." That's because when there's a great piece of dialogue, I put it in the bank and find a better place for it.

Is it all shot in English, will it be dubbed?

In Germany, yes, and in France I believe they're gonna show it both ways.

Are the Italians in it as well?

I don't know all the deals. I don't know which deals are closed and which are open.

In Europe when you say producer you mean the person who is also in charge of the whole financing deals.

Yeah, you see that's what the French company which hired me, is actually doing.

So you're not in there with your company.

That's the way it always is. The Levinson/Fontana company gets hired by Warner Brothers, but we don't do financing.

You don't risk in any way neither in the development phase nor later. That is very different from the European model, you know. When you say to European writers, You have to become a producer what we think is that we will have to raise the money, defer our fees, at least partly, cover the deficit, risk.

What I mean is producer in the American model…the producer is responsible for the cost, maintains the cost of the production. In other words you agreed a budget and you work to keep to that budget, that's your job.

I heard Bill Goldman talking the other day, and he said something that really impressed me. He said, I don't like my writing, I never like my writing. Do you like your writing?

No, no! I hate my writing. It's very funny he says that because when I get it down on paper I go like, "No, that's not good enough," I always think it could be better. The hardest part for me when watching an episode of *St. Elsewhere* or *Homicide* or *Oz* is, I'll go, "Oh shit, now I know how to write that scene." Because as you go through life you get better at it. Hopefully you get better at it. I'll tell you a very quick story, I was at Elaine's restaurant, and there were three writers and I, and one of the writers who worked for *Law & Order*, said to the other three of us, "Did you see last week's episode of *Law & Order*?" And we all said, "No." And he said, "It was maybe one of the greatest hours of television ever." So he talked about it and we were all like, "That sounds great." And I said, "So who wrote it?" He said, "I did." He leaves and the other three of us are still drinking, and I say, "Have you ever liked anything you've ever written?" And they're all like, "No! We were so shocked at his sense of greatness."

Well, he's blessed. Most writers are insecure.

Well, the great lesson that I learned doing episodic television is, you can keep working on it up to a point and then you have to stop. 'Cause they have to shoot it, and then you have to edit it. So you have to stop, there comes a moment where you have to say, "That's as good as it's gonna be." The upside of episodic television is you can say, "I have next week, I can get it right next week, I'll start anew. I learned what I did wrong in this episode so next week's episode will be so much better."

You wrote theater plays, you wrote TV movies and series, you wrote documentaries. What is your favorite form?

I love doing TV series, because I like the kind of novelesque nature of TV to take the character on a journey over the course of five years. Having said that, I think that if I get an idea and it's a haiku, I'll write the haiku. Certain things should be plays and certain things should be TV shows and certain things should be movies and certain things should be radio plays and certain things should be an epic poem. And the other thing is I love to write. I consider it a blessing that I get to write every single morning, and at some point I won't be able to do it anymore so I want to write everything right now. Because my ability to write will end and before it ends I want to be able to say I got it all done. I like writing. I'm not a poet, that's the one thing I can't do.

You don't use the computer at all, is that right?

I write long hand and then I give the pages to Kate and Larry (Tom's assistants). You know what, there is a sensuality to this (he mimics writing with a pen), that this (he mimics writing on a computer) doesn't have. I don't know, I don't get turned on by a keyboard. The other thing is you want to do that (he scrambles a piece of paper on his desk and throws it across the room). I would be throwing computers across the room like every ten minutes. (laughs) That's why I don't get a computer, it would be too expensive. And, on a computer the scene looks so finished, and it's spell-checked and it looks so done, and a first draft should never look done, it shouldn't look nice, it should look horrible. Working on a computer is too clean and orderly. Writing is chaos, writing is anarchy, don't you think?

I just can't imagine not working on a computer anymore.

There's only a couple of us left. I know David Kelley still writes long hand.

Amazing. Tell me about the writers you used on Borgia.

I took on writers I have worked with before, so we could cut through a lot of stuff. In the first year of a series, it's important to know who the players are. After that you can start to experiment. As I said, I don't know anyone on the crew, I only knew two of the actors prior to shooting and I didn't know any of the directors, I mean that's a huge amount of risk for me, placing the baby in the hands of strangers. But I've been very lucky. I mean, Oliver Hirschbiegel – we respect each other so much. I kept waiting for the ceiling to fall – but it never did. (laughs)

What about your writers? Were they with you on set?

There's always a writer on set. Right now Brant Englestein, one of our story editors, is there, while I'm here. Kyle Bradstreet, one of our other story editors is going soon too. It's important to have a writer on the set, to be able to listen to the dialogue and know that the scene is working. Because in television, things happen so fast it's really important for a writer to be around and say, "Now here's the intention of the scene," because without our active participation, my instinct is to overwrite the scene and to make it very obvious what the scene is about. To me, that's the worst kind of writing, because it has no subtlety. That's what a writer needs to do when he's not on set, and that makes for bad TV.

That's a great point you're making there.

And, you know, what's funny is each director the first couple of days, is like, "Why is he coming up to me?" And then they go, "Oh, this is actually a conversation." One of the *Borgia* directors actually said to me that he'd never had this kind of experience before, you know, that he can turn to the writer and say, "This is it, right, we got it?" I think he's had a bit of a revelation, this is a good thing.

Way to go.

Sometimes, there's so much going during filming, the director is looking at something else or is working with the DP, and I'm sitting at the monitor and all I have to do is watch.

What about directing yourself?

No. I could hire myself to direct anytime I want. But I would never hire me.

Why?

I'm not a visual. If you say to me, that's ten feet away, I do not have the capacity to say what ten feet is. I'm a writer and a writer thinks the way a writer thinks. That's not to say there are a lot of great writer-directors. But I also think it's really good to let the script go. Of course, I can let it go because I know I'll get it back.

That's another great thing you said right there.

Plus I get final cut.

You get final cut?!

I always have final cut.

That's amazing. I haven't heard that from other showrunners.

I don't know.

I always ask and they say no, not contractually. But practically that's how it works.

Ultimately, in America, if the network says this episode is unacceptable, the studio can cut it. Because if they don't deliver the episode they're in breach of their contract, so technically, the studio and the network can take it away from me, but creatively I have the final cut.

It's not the director?

Not the director.

So you edit here in New York and you edit without Oliver?

Oliver did his cut. He did a director's cut.

In Prague?

Yes. And now I'm working on it.

And that's fine with him?

(laughs) So far.

Is there anything I haven't covered, Tom, which you think is important?

The only thing that I would add, and this is a very non-Hollywood point of view, I think it's essential for us writers to write what is important to us, what touches us, what makes us laugh and not try to please everybody else. And that isn't to say you don't want to please everybody else, I want everyone to love everything I've ever written, but I think that what happens in Hollywood, and I don't know whether it happens in Europe as well, I think people look to being successful as opposed to being faithful. And when I say faithful I mean faithful to themselves and to the truth within them. And I think it's very easy for that to get lost in the need to be successful, in the "Oh, I want the trophies, I want the money, I want the car, I want the house" way. And I only say that having been seduced by that and then having woken up and said, "Well, wait a minute, is that really what I wanted out of being a writer?" So I probably could have had a more successful career because there were several times when I chose to not do what was commercially the wisest choice. I feel like I have been faithful and therefore, because I have been continually faithful to the writing, I don't feel the need to be successful in my career. That allows me the freedom to be able to invite other people into the dance. You know what I mean? But it's easy to lose that, especially in our business.

If you would rewind the clock and go 20 years back, would you do something differently?

I don't think I would. Let me put it this way. There are things that I wish I could have done better. But it isn't like "oh, I should have taken that job on that Spielberg movie", I don't have those kind of regrets. There are moments when you say, I could have done that better and I wish I had it back.

Why don't you do more movies?

I'll tell you what. I've done rewrites on movies. I've never been in awe of movies, the way many people are. To me, telling the story, exploring characters, defining the times we live – that's what it's about, and if I can do it on TV and have the freedom I get, why would I trade that to write a movie where I'm gonna be shit on because screenwriters are notoriously shit on by directors? What do I need it for? Also right now the movies that are being made…I don't have an interest in them.

But why don't people like you reverse this?

Because then I'd have to get into raising the money. And I'm too busy raising the money for the Writers Guild of America East Foundation. (laughs)

Jenny Bicks

Jenny Bicks has written and was an executive producer for the HBO series *Sex and the City*, for which she won numerous Golden Globe and Emmy awards, and is currently a writer and executive producer for *The Big C*. She is also the creator and writer of the ABC series *Men in Trees* and wrote the screenplay for the 2003 film *What a Girl Wants*.

You wrote for your first series in 1993. What brought you there? What did you study, what was your background?

That's good that you actually found my whole thing back to '93! I graduated from a small college with a degree in English Literature and worked in advertising for five years in New York City. And then ended up getting a job on a sitcom in 1993, that was *It Had to Be You* with Faye Dunaway. It was a very rare combination because she'd never done a sitcom before. I just figured, it's my first job, I'm so lucky and I moved out to California to work on that. I then proceeded to work on six or seven sitcoms (among them were *The 5 Mrs. Buchanans, The Naked Truth, Almost Perfect, Leap of Faith*) and the movie *What a Girl Wants* for the next couple of years, some better than others. Most people didn't know them and they didn't last very long, perhaps 17 episodes, which wasn't even a full year. But I got trained in sitcom, in story and in working in a writers' room because at that time sitcom TV was at a peak, so they were spending a lot of money and they were filling their rooms with writers, so I had a chance to work in rooms of, well, mainly men, I mean it was usually myself and a bunch of guys.

This hasn't changed that much, has it?

(laughs) No, that has not changed. It still is that way. It was great for me to learn the structure of a joke there. The single-camera comedy didn't exist – single-camera was for one hour and more, or for cable. The first time I worked on a one-hour show was in a show called *Dawson's Creek*, which doesn't exist anymore. Then I went on to *Sex and the City*, where I worked for six years. And that was pretty much the thing that trained me in story breaking, in story writing (note: Jenny wrote 15 episodes from 1998 to 2004). We like to think that *Sex and the City* was the thing that brought half-hour single-camera comedy into the consciousness of television. Then I created *Men in Trees*, which was a one-hour show for ABC, and that was all for two years, and then I came on to *The Big C*, which is where I am now. This is our second season, and it is a half-hour single-camera. We call it comedy but it's taken that form of comedy now, that is both very dramatic and very comedic. We have kind of reframed what comedy means.

You talked about going into a writers' room in a sitcom. When and how did that concept start?

Writers' rooms existed already back in the 50s. These old comic legends, three or four of these guys would be in rooms together. And I think it evolved from there. What happened there was that in the 80s and 90s, the rooms grew bigger, you went from having three or four writers in a room to 15 writers. They were called from different places and being put in a room. The writers' room was originally meant for comedians to try out their jokes and material. And the rooms I was in ... that was still what was happening. You would throw a joke out there and see if it got a response. Each room went a bit differently, depending on who the showrunner was and how he liked to do it but generally it was about bouncing off each other jokes and stories, trying to get the room to laugh, that became significant ... You know, if you can get the room to laugh, then it is worth investigating.

Did you have a writers' room in Sex and the City *and how did that work?*

The writers' room there was very small. When we started that show, there were three of us. When we finished we had six people in there and that felt very big to us. We spent a lot of time in the room at the beginning of each season, really marking out the arcs of where we wanted these characters to start and finish, for each of the characters in *Sex and the City*. Making sure that these arcs worked well with each other, laying them out on a board, making sure that the peaks didn't hit at the same time ... It's like composing a score, you want to figure out which of your instruments is playing more strongly at what time. So we would spend a very long time in the room and then we would break each episode and also spend a lot of time together, talking about story ... That is still how I do it now. And even when I did my one-hour, *Men in Trees*, I believe this is what we did: really mapping out at the very beginning where you want things to start and end. Generally you decide what you want your first and last image to be, for each season. For instance, that's what we are doing right now. We just sorted the writers' room in *The Big C* three weeks ago. We spent the first week to ten days building these bigger arcs, then we started to break the first four episodes. We will do the bigger arc, then go into each episode, and each episode will be the job of one writer. For instance today we'll be talking about Episodes Three and Four, trying to put things on the board, talk about them, the beats of each story, make sure they work inside each story but also in the big picture and in the context of what came before, in the prior episode.

And then each writer goes off and writes her first draft?

Basically the way I do it and I think it's very common to work this way ... at *Sex and the City* we used to call it the independent study ... each writer takes care of her own episode, from start to finish. So she would go away at this point and start to write an outline, after it was broken down, an outline scene by scene, what happens in each scene. Then (as a showrunner) I'll take it back into the room and I will take comments from the room and then give notes to the writer, of what I think, which notes they should address and which they shouldn't. They'll go away, write their script and the same thing will happen, a script will come back into the room, everybody will read it, give notes, and then we'll make the changes, and only then will it go to the studio and then to the network.

How many drafts are we talking about?

Well, it depends on time. At the beginning we have plenty of time to do more. Certainly you do two drafts, perhaps three, if you consider the studio draft and the network draft as two separate drafts. There are times when you do not have that amount of time. There were times when I had to take a script and make changes superquick. Ideally we'll have a draft from the room, go to the room and make changes, then we'll go to the studio and they'll make changes, then we'll go to the network and they'll make changes.

Are there cases where as a showrunner you will have to change most of what the original writer wrote?

That's very rare. I think last season we had one case, and it wasn't the writer's fault; occasionally there's a story that doesn't work in script form, you hope that doesn't happen and you'll figure that out before you get to script and then we took the script apart and each writer took a scene and once I've also taken a whole script and rewritten it. But it's not useful for me to spend my time doing that. Certainly, there's some shows where the head writer will take more on. They will take and rewrite all scripts.

I understand that the idea is that the series has one voice, that one has the feeling that it is written by one person.

I will do that as a note that I give to the writer as opposed to polishing each one. I also believe – and this again is the training that I got on *Sex and the City* – that a show works best if there is more than a singular voice, and that a different aspect of each character gets represented by each writer. If you watch *Sex and the City*, you'll notice that each episode feels maybe a little different. I know which writer wrote it, because it is perhaps a bit more cynical, more of a cynical side of Miranda, more this kind of Carrie, and in the end it's the different characters but it's not one voice. It's one voice with different angles.

This is very interesting. I really like what you're saying here. It seems to correspond to the collaborative nature of the writers' room in the best possible way – as a method to achieving different perspectives of the personalities of the characters. Now, apart from the size of the writers' room are there any other differences between drama and sitcom? Would you say that there is a different kind of development or collaboration between the writers? Or in the way the rooms are structured?

It's a good question. I haven't been in a sitcom room, say, since the late 90s and maybe things have changed. You wanted to melt your voice as much as possible with the showrunner's voice. You wanted to make the showrunner happy and you wanted to be a real good mimic. What happens in drama is that it is more important that you know structurally how to do a script. Maybe that's also because I have been working more in cable in the last ten years than I have in network. There is much more structure, especially if it is a one-hour. Especially now because most networks want you to have six acts, as every commercial break creates an act, so you are constantly writing to a big moment, that they can go out on, which is very false. That's a long way of saying, I think the difference is that you are less worried in sitcom about structure and more worried about getting a joke and in drama you are more worried about the serialized nature of your characters and the structure of your script. That might not be fair to say anymore for a sitcom, though, as I haven't been in one in a while.

What about content and material? Are cable and network not more and more close to each other?

I have to say that it continues to be an issue for network that they just won't touch certain areas and that we're not allowed to explore certain areas. It's interesting because I'm writing this show for Showtime but it's

Sony Television for Showtime. So Sony is our studio. Sony does mainly network television. So sometimes the notes that I will get from them are network notes, meaning things like, how are we going to be sure we like this character? There is more concern in network that people will not like your character, and that he is likeable. Especially if it's a woman. So, you can give them flaws but you have to be very careful. There's a sense still in cable in general, that your characters can be very powerful and very flawed, and you really can't do that in network. There is still a desire in network to have a beginning, middle and end, so there's a kind of wrap-up in every episode, while in cable you do not have to have the character learn a lesson or have the character come full circle, you know, to tie it all up with a bow. In cable we're allowed to just be with our characters, we can have them make huge mistakes and not necessarily learn from them. That's still an issue with network. You know, network has not really grown as much as you would expect, based on all the successes happening in cable. I was surprised that when I came back into network for a little while, after I had done *Sex and the City* for six years, they hadn't really learned from the success of *Sex and the City* or *The Sopranos*. I don't believe they trust the American viewer. People know what they like to watch, but they don't give them enough credit.

It's basically the taste of a few people which determines what the audience is going to watch, right? They are like gatekeepers. And as you said, mainly men. But don't they change and go from cable to network and back, for one thing?

They're starting to do that more and more, and that's good. Bob Greenblatt, who ran Showtime and was the person who shepherded *The Big C*, along with *Weeds* and *Nurse Jackie*, a bunch of shows about these very strong, very flawed women...he just moved over to NBC. And that's a huge change for us. In general that hasn't happened much. You have these...well, mainly men who have these jobs in networks and they keep moving up and they'll all stay in studio network world. There are writers who are going back and forth so you got to have these guys who are making the decisions crossing back and forth too, right? For instance, Paul Lee, who is now running ABC here, he took Steve McPherson's job, and is British: he is already bringing a kind of sensibility to the kind of shows he wants, that has never been here before. It is still amazing how much power a couple of people have. And it never ceases to amaze me that the people who are in charge of comedy have not one stick of humor in them. When you meet with them, you just wonder why they are the people choosing what's gonna be the next funny thing out there. I think more and more or certainly I hear more and more that over the next year or two, they'll be starting a system that's based more in trusting the showrunner to come in and do what they're good at as opposed to telling them what the network needs. So perhaps that will bring more of a vision. It means that basically the showrunner can come in and say, you know what I am fascinated by, Sarah Palin, I'm amazed how conservative politics have taken a strong hold, and I really want to write a show about that. And rather than them saying, "great but could it be based in a bakery" (laughs), they would say, "That seems to be really interesting and that is what he can do well, so go on and do it."

Does each showrunner have his own production company?

I have my own production company but it's really in vanity name only. Nobody is financing their own shows. Even as a production company I have to have a studio, that will finance what I want to make and then we'll go together to a network, so we all depend on a studio and a network in terms of what they will finance. Maybe Dick Wolf ... and I'm not sure he does this either. If you want to get paid for development you're going to go in business with a studio, which is going to give you a development deal and then you get to develop with them.

So basically you have both network and studio executives at the table when you're talking story?

You develop it first with your studio collaborators, with the people who are actually financing you as the writer, you will pitch that idea to them, you will work with them. In a case like Sony, when they don't have a deal with just one network ... This is one of the things that happened in the last ten years, vertical integration where basically every studio has a network, so if you're having a deal with ABC studios you're going to go pitch to ABC. And if they don't want it you can go somewhere else but it's difficult to sell somewhere else. Sony can sell anywhere. But such companies are more rare now than ever. Most are in business with one network.

As a writer who loves writing, do you prefer to be the showrunner or a writer in the writers' room?

You know the ideal, even as a showrunner, is to be in the room. This isn't true of all showrunners maybe, but because I'm raised in sitcom rooms I like collaboration, I like talking, I like to be able to develop stories together. There are certainly days where as a showrunner you would much prefer to not be the showrunner. Because making the decisions and having to have that kind of pressure on you beyond just being in a room and creating, it's...it's a pain in the ass, and sometimes you just don't want that kind of responsibility, you wanna be what we call the number two. That's the person underneath the showrunner who has plenty of power but doesn't have to make the final decisions. He can be just writer.

Do you see an evolution in formats? I mean is there a specific trend right now?

Right now networks are very pro half-hour single-camera comedy. That was not always the case. Single-camera, when I started, end of the 90s, was for one-hour drama or for cable, not network.

Cable had started as the place where you did not need ratings because there was no advertising. But they do pay attention to ratings now, don't they?

They matter but as they do not use them as a sales tool at cable, it doesn't change the numbers how many people watch the show or not. *Mad Men* gets a tiny audience on AMC but it has a lot of critical acclaim, so there's a trade-off.

So you're saying that they may keep something because it's good for prestige reasons.

Yeah. This makes them able and willing to take chances. They're looking for subscribers. So they are looking for attention and publicity. People will watch the Golden Globes, and will say, *Boardwalk Empire*, what's that show? And suddenly they'll subscribe. They're really looking to enhance their subscriber base more than anything else. And certainly internationally and that's part of what they are about. That they will get programming that will appeal to Germany or to Italy as much as it appeals to the US audiences.

Are there other trends, especially because of the internet?

You know, what is interesting is, that maybe five years ago, people thought that the internet would create a lot of bonanza for programming. I don't think that that has happened yet. I mean, people create web series, but I don't think that anyone has figured out how to make money on that. And it certainly hasn't created programming on cable or network that is shorter. There are a couple of things that came from the internet. Like *Web Therapy*, which is a show that Lisa Kudrow does, that started on the internet and now is on Showtime. But beyond that they stayed very classical in how they tell story. There is a trend at HBO towards miniseries, that is, towards short-term series, which is great. That is eight episodes or so, and that's it. HBO has explored this a lot, Showtime less so.

Are the budgets going up? There are some shows where the budgets seem huge.

Yes, they are spending money. HBO has always been a huge spender. They will spend more than any other network, cable or otherwise, spends. But even half-hour single-camera comedy is significantly more expensive than a sitcom. They are spending for production.

How does a showrunner decide whom to invite into a room? How does he choose his number two, how does he choose the other writers?

It's a combination of a lot of things. First you look at what show you're writing and what kind of experience you want for that type of show. I personally like to choose people I have worked with before, because it's important; the writers' room is a little corporation, you have to make sure that everybody gets along with everybody, that you curate the room correctly. So you ask yourself first, whom do I know who could do this well? Then you go to, what kind of person do we want to do this? For instance, on this show we wanted to avoid going typical. Would we want, for instance, playwrights, people who do not have a lot of experience with TV but work well with character? Because when you're trained within a certain system for too long, you take on some bad habits. If you're good with sitcom, you can't necessarily make a great character-based show. So you read a lot of material, you meet people. You need to find people who are willing to be very open about their lives, technically they have to draw (off) from their lives, who seem to play well with others, who collaborate well. Sometimes you don't know, you put them in a room, and you have to see.

You have done a lot of shows with female characters. Are writers also typecast like actors? Has this happened to you as a writer or was it always your own choice to focus on a certain kind of show?

Trust me, I don't want anything else. I have certain strengths and I am not getting pursued for other stuff. There are other people who are specialized in other things. I wouldn't do crime series, I cannot do espionage series, I'm not that person. So I guess the answer is both. One could say that I have been to some extent pigeonholed, because I wanted to be. I think we write best what we know. So I don't have trouble with that. What I have trouble with, is if people would say, she can't write men. Because that will happen. I like writing relationships – not necessarily romantic relationships – and this has put me in the romantic comedy world. Also in movies. I tend to write romantic comedies.

So what about writing for the movies versus TV?

This is something I do do. I only have one movie actually produced. It was a movie called *What a Girl Wants*, I wrote it maybe 15 years ago. It was a remake of a movie called *The Reluctant Debutante*, a movie from the 50s. It is a good example of the differences between writing for the movies and writing for TV. It was the first movie I ever wrote. I was lucky because I didn't actually have a movie spec to show them, and by the time it was shot, maybe ten years after I wrote it, there had probably been eight writers that had worked on that project. It went from being a personal little movie about a girl in her twenties who goes to London to a very straight-ahead girl movie about a 16-year old girl who goes to London: that changed everything. It's really about the writer being a conduit to the project as opposed to the writer being in charge. And I've been lucky to have actually done enough movies now where people know what I bring to the process. Generally writers are tossed aside. Whether it's good or bad, once you produced that thing it gets handed over to the director and it's the director who's the showrunner. I've been lucky to have worked with directors who were collaborative and valued what I have to say but usually the thing is that they take it and make it what they want. In TV the writer is king. I try very hard now to only work with producers in movies who know who I am and who want to work with me. I've set it up that way. Unless I need cash. (laughs) I am also a script doctor so I can make money easily editing scripts. But I don't see that as art. Generally in movies it goes like that: oh, we don't like this draft, well, let's hire another writer. Which I think is a mistake, not just ego-wise but also in terms of creating a singular voice.

People do tend to say that there is no crossover between writers for TV and writers for movies. You end up being one or the other. Would you agree?

Not really. Working on a cable show as I do now I have more time anyway. This is the second season we are shooting here at *The Big C*, and it's 13 episodes. It's not 22 or 24. I have a long period of time, you know, about half of my year, where I won't be doing this. So I can work on movie screenplays.

There seem to be shows where each episode is being directed by a different director.

Well, over the last three years or so it has been established that there is one main director on each show. A director who will direct more than anyone else. And who'll also be there to help shepherd the other directors who come in. The truth is that when you have directors who are cycling in and cycling out, there is no sense of what is the show. You don't want the show to look completely different every week. The other thing we do is called "crossboarding", which means you shoot two episodes at the same time. So you're not having a new person every five days, but we take two shows and we prep and shoot them together.

How many projects do you actually have at all times, which are developed up to a certain point?

There is a lot of change in the last few years concerning this. It used to be that you'd get these big development deals. I don't think that this was necessarily such a good idea. You would get a lot of money and then they would pick an idea or two and you would lie low and they would go and sell, for it to get produced. It wasn't economically a very smart model for them. So what happened was that the development deals got smaller money-wise. They also started to reach out for spec projects, which are out there. Like this season they will pick more scripts which people wrote on their own. What that means is that the writer gets to show what their vision is before it gets attached to a studio. The people who were mostly successful in doing that were writers that they know, writers who can be showrunners. So they bring in a project that is already packaged. Here it is, I'll run it, if you like the script. Sometimes they bring in a director as well. I will personally have eight or nine ideas, in my head or in my computer somewhere, and I know I want to create a show of them at some point. Whether I'll write all of those or I'll develop them before I find the right person to work with on them, I don't know. There was a time when they were spending a lot of money on big names, David Kelley or Aaaron Sorkin, for instance – and they are great entities. They are now kind of spreading the wealth a little bit more and spend the money also on up and coming showrunners rather than on people who will cost them seven or eight million a year. The economics have changed, they are not spending as much money. And there are a lot of feature writers now that are crossing into TV. For a while it was us going to movies, now there are movie guys coming in and writing pilots.

How about The Big C? *You did not create this show, is that right?*

Right. This is actually the first time I run a show that I didn't create. And that is definitely a mixed bag. We've managed to actually work pretty well together. Darleen, who created the show, is an actress, and she knew that her strength is character.

So it is not a one-way thing where you become a creator and you cannot go back?

Yes you can, but I am also lucky because I reached this point in my career where I can do whatever I want. This show was great and I wanted to do cable again and I had some personal history with cancer. People get driven by this desire to win a Golden Globe, but I don't need more awards. We don't have to repeat it.

You are a very lucky person for being able to appreciate this, actually, and to not have to repeat it.

Trust me, I know that. Write what you know, write what you want to write, go towards the love. That is what I tell all the writers. The thing you are attracted to, you will do.

The award is creative freedom, right? And that is the place where you will create your best material.

Absolutely. *Sex and the City* was that place. We loved it. We loved working with each other, we loved writing these characters, we loved these voices. The success was just the icing. And if you can find a situation like that you are very lucky. And then you get the award, great. But you can't write something because you think, Oh this is gonna get me that. 'Cause I've done that and it bit me in the ass.

Is working in a writers' room like siblings competing for mother's love?

So much is changing right now, in terms of form vs content but one thing isn't changing: it is still incredibly tough to be a woman in this business. I'm very fortunate that I've gone past that place where people will judge me, but a lot of women get stopped at a certain point, and they do get pigeonholed, it's a business that is led by men. I wish that were different, and I think that has to be said because it is something we are all fighting against.

Any suggestions?

What I try to do in my small way as a showrunner, is to hire women and to give women more chances to move up. To show that women can do that as well. There are sitcom writers' rooms of colleagues that have no women at all. I wish they would realize that women are funny. And that they can do the job just as well. I say that publicly too: I think women are better suited to be showrunners than men. I think we have an ability to multitask. They've done all these tests on men's brains which show that they are capable to compartmentalize – but we are better diplomats, we hear people. When I am in a restaurant I am listening to the conversations around me…Men sometimes become so set on their vision that they can't even see what's around them. And, frankly, I think the more of us who run shows and run them well, the better.

Robert Carlock

Robert Carlock was the showrunner of *30 Rock*, together with Tina Fey. Before that, he was on the writing staff of *Saturday Night Live* (*SNL*) from 1996 to 2001 and *Friends* from 2001 to 2004. He has won, among others, three Emmy awards, three Producers' Guild awards, six Writers' Guild awards, a Peabody award, a Television Critics Association award, a GLAAD award and a Golden Globe.

So how did you get to running a show?

There's no direct line to get here. People come from all over the place, but I probably had the most boring route, at least in comedy, which is: I worked for the Harvard Lampoon, that's the comedy magazine at Harvard.[1] I joined it as an undergraduate. I come from a family with a lot of journalists and advertising people and painters, so I joined it to hang out with like-minded people. And then you realize that all people who leave here go do *this* for a living. I was always a fan of *Saturday Night Live* so in a panic, not having any other skills as a history and literature major, and not wanting to go into academia, I started trying to write. I came out at a lucky time in the life of comedy. There was a lot of comedy on TV. In the mid 1990s there were something like 40 sitcoms on TV, half-hour shows, and the whole Late Night world. And I was able to get an agent right out of college and a good one too, and get myself read. Soon I was on a prime time sketch comedy show (The Dana Carvey Show), that further drove the nail in the coffin of prime time sketch comedy. (laughs) That didn't work for whatever reason, and then I went to *SNL*.

So you got an agent before you had a job. That is pretty unusual today.

Yes, the agents back then were looking for clients, which is just not the case today. Anyway, compared with the Second City people, doing stand-up and all that, which is quite a different skill set and background, my story is a little dry. But I've been lucky to work since then.

You basically learned writing on the job.

Yeah. I learned writing for performance. You know, I had been writing mildly humored essays and things, and I spent time with some really funny people. A lot of what we do is sitting in a room and sharing jokes. And it's not meant to be competitive because you're all pointing towards the same goal, making the script as good as it can be, but still... you know everyone is a little bit keeping score at the back of their head, who is contributing, who is the funniest, you feel like I want to be able to fit in. *SNL* is a very exciting, very competitive place to work. Live things are such a thrill and so hard to get these days. There are some great sketch writers who stay there for a very long time but I didn't want to, I wanted to write stories, so I left and went to *Friends* for three years.

How was that?

It was great. It feels like I came at the very end of the life of the show, I was just a staff writer and grew up to producer there, so I was still learning. But to be honest, I don't think that show ever got the credit it deserved in terms of the storytelling and the complexity of storytelling. In reality it was very serious about the shape of stories and stories interconnecting in the best episodes, which is something I really like to do. There's some kind of a gloss on that show, everyone's so pretty and life is so easy in that sort of fictional New York that they created...so they never got the respect it deserved for the writing. It was great to sit with these people and to see how they construct stories and the questions that they ask about stories. I try to do the same here at *30 Rock*, I ask the writers very specific questions: is this satisfying? Is it developing? Is it moving the story forward? – and there are often very interesting answers to that. For instance, Ross in *Friends* might be spending his time with a guest cast member, and is never checking in with his people, but that's what people hook into of course – the interaction between the friends. And you are asking yourself why didn't the table-read or the rehearsal feel as satisfying as it should have. Often you have to take something apart and put it back together or completely change it. Which we did a lot with *Friends*. Sometimes, if a story wasn't working, we threw it out completely.

Did you have a writers' room at SNL?

At *SNL* you are left to your own devices. It is once a week that all writers meet. It tends to be the case with variety. Everyone is dumping their ideas into the big pot. They're just pulling out 50 things at the big table read each Wednesday, each of which has individual initials or names at the top of it...Then 11 or 12 get produced and eight or nine of them get aired on television that week.

So the writers decide together?

The producers decide. It's just a less collaborative process, out of necessity, and also, because of the nature of the beast, a more competitive process. The whole point of the variety show is that it's a lot of different voices, while a sitcom has to have a single voice. So a balanced *SNL* show is a lot of people with different voices and a lot of people getting excluded from week to week. Which means that the writers' room there is much less important and different than at a sitcom. Out of necessity, for survival, performers need to team up with writers, and writers of course need the strength of that performer's voice to get their material heard, so there's constant collaboration between writers and performers. But in terms of the group effort, that is so essential to a sitcom ... At *SNL* and most variety shows there is no incentive to be helpful at a table read. At *SNL* you'd be writing someone else's thing for them to get the full credit, and that makes for a different experience. *SNL* has a staff in order to cull as many individual voices as possible. While here we put together a staff, to try to have a diversity of voices – but then we melt them together to produce a varied but distinctive singular voice, that is hopefully very close to something that Tina (Fey) wants it to be.

How many writers are in the room at 30 Rock?

Including Tina, I think we're 13 this year. At *Friends* it was between 12 and 14 in the few years I was there. What that number allows you to do, which is sort of crucial, is to split into two groups. A lot of the work is done with everybody, you want everyone's opinion when a script comes in, or if a script is being pitched before it is being written, you need to be able to count on everybody knowing what each script is about. But to maximize your efficiency you split into two groups, and one group may be working on a script which is shooting in two weeks and another group is working on creating the stories for the script after that. When we started, because Tina and I didn't want to split groups as we were creating that tone we were talking about, we had an eight- or nine-person staff, and with Tina acting, someone watching on stage as a producer, we weren't splitting much. That was intentional because at the time we all educated ourselves in terms of what the show wanted to be.

So you or Tina or both are always in the writers' room?

Yeah, and of course Tina's situation is unique, I think, as she is working almost every day as an actor. So a lot of what I am doing is trying to pull her in so she can be there at touchstone moments. When I am pitching something I am pitching it to Tina. One of the ancillary groups comes up with a story and they come to me and we work on it. But then, if it's something that we want to do, we sort of lay it out step by step, and it's on the boards, and then I take it to Tina and find her in her crazy, busy life and pitch it to her, and she may have suggestions. In most shows there isn't that stuff of going to find the actress, but she isn't the actress really, she is a writer-producer. I also go to pitch things to Alec because I like to keep him informed and if we're doing something with the character I definitely want him to understand where we're coming from, before he sees it on the page. So I'm sending off the writers to do work that always bubbles back through me. There's a hierarchy of seniority: there's certain people who will take a room, certain people who are learning to take a room and people who are staff writers.

What do you mean "take the room"?

To run it.

And report back to you?

Yes, at the end of the day or at the end of a couple of days. Usually every day we sit down with the top writer-producers.

Can you walk me through the development of a script?

The platonic version, which doesn't happen often, but then it does to a fair amount, is you're in the room and someone is giving guidance to that room, let's say it's me. So you're saying this is what we're left with at the end of the last season, and you want to try to focus on the next step in the larger story. By now hopefully you're broken into these smaller rooms, let's say it's me and four other people, and you just talk through it. Then you put it on the board and see how it looks like. You look at the outline, then you probably call the other room in and share that with them and make your adjustments. We are used to doing three or four stories for an episode...

And each story is connected with a different character, right?

Yes. This is Jack's story, he needs to be doing this because he's just had a baby... That sort of thing. I'm a big believer in stories trying to inter-connect. So we talk about the A story, the B story and the runner – we often find ourselves having two A stories, a B story and a runner. I'm a big believer in the runner – because it's often four or five comic beats, and it's not impactful emotionally.

Will you give me a definition for the runner?

It's usually about one of the co-characters. It's the least emotionally impactful story, but often a purely comic story, and for that reason, because it doesn't have a lot of shape to it, it's usually the shortest. I tend to think of it as a little release valve. If you're telling two weighty stories, you can then turn away to that silly little thing. We tend to overwrite so our runners are not the classic four- or five-beat story. Here (points to a dry erase board in his office that has an outlined episode on it) we have one with seven beats... Then we pitch this out to Tina and get her notes and get her approval and then we assign it to a writer. With an outline or a beat sheet. Breaking a story or an episode is like breaking a wild horse, I guess... (laughs)

That is a fun metaphor! Are we still in the platonic version?

Yes, we are. So the writer or the writing team would write an outline and in an ideal world they would have four or five days for that task. In the beginning of the year things are more slow, and that's a document I try to keep around six pages, but more often we end up writing around seven or eight pages. It basically just describes the scenes, some of the jokes; we really just try to track the narrative threads and show how these things connect.

So it is the first time where you actually have a timeline, where you see how the stories play in time, how they interconnect?

Well, one of the things we do before that, we go to a numbered order of the scenes.

So it's an easy job for the writers, is it?

It's all there, and they still screw it up. (laughs) And you go through things like, now here is where the day changes etc., and sometimes you're wrong – you learn so much at each of these stages. In the effort to move forward sometimes you miss things that don't add up, or things that repeat themselves. And when you ask them to turn this into pages, they might realize it is a lot and they come back confused and they have questions. We always have a dialogue, as they're working on the outline. And usually I do a rewrite on the outline, before giving it to Tina. We then send the outline to the studio/network for their approval. So there will be notes on the outline.

Can somebody who doesn't write actually read an outline and understand it?

That's a very good question. A lot of times explaining something small may take more space than explaining a complicated emotional story. And often we will hear that: it seems that this light story is taking up too much weight. And I always find that when we go to script it becomes again what it's supposed to be. But to explain "someone buys a new hat" takes as much time as to explain "someone's mother died" – so it may feel like there's an imbalance. It's a very good question. The executives are aware that they're not the writers, and some are better than others. We've been very lucky. I mean it's tough, but I think at this point in the life of the show our executives know the show so well and its tone, that they don't ask the questions that they used to ask. At the same time it can be annoying to have a separate party who doesn't do what we do, to have opinions – but if you think of them as an audience...

But an audience will see the actual film, it's different. They will not read something which is still on its way there.

Of course. Look, good executives are better than bad executives.

I'll quote you on that.

(laughs) When we have doubts about something... For instance, two years ago we were ending a season, Tina's character Liz wanted to have a baby, and we ended the year with "I'm gonna try to adopt." And the way we did it in that final episode is, we jumped three months ahead in everyone's story. We had a plan for the next year, how it would play out and how it would help put a pin in that larger story of Liz. But when we shot it, we had little nagging doubts and the network gave us notes, like "Is that too crazy?", "Is that a weird place to leave Liz?" They were worried about leaving Liz all summer with that, they were concerned. So we discussed that. But to go back to what happens... The outline is approved, the writer gets notes and goes off to write a first draft. And, as you know as a writer, when you write a draft coming off of an outline, you discover mistakes. It's so easy in an outline but now you have to dramatize it or find a reason why someone says or does something. Often the network will ask, well, what is the real purpose of the scene? So in the outline we try to make it incredibly clear, forget the jokes, and make clear what the character is thinking and feeling right now, that relates him or her to the scene before and after. So the draft may come back, and it doesn't work. It doesn't make sense.

What doesn't work?

I guess when you have 20 minutes to tell a story, you have to be very concise or get away with being a little less concise. There isn't room or time for the luxury of scenes that don't move the story forward. If a scene isn't giving you new information and people aren't in it with clear attitudes, there's something wrong. Maybe the scene structure is wrong or maybe the wrong people are talking to each other.

Do you think in terms of acts?

What we usually try to do is indicate where we think act breaks are coming. We usually write three acts, yeah. But, to be perfectly honest, we often find the breaks in editing. Because NBC insists on two breaks, and it used to be that one of these breaks was your main titles, but then they wanted the story after the main titles to keep the audience, which makes sense – and that enforced a three-act structure. But some episodes want to be two acts, or some stories want to be two acts within the same episode and some want to be three... A runner is like a one-acter; there isn't an act break in a runner. From a story point of view, there should be act breaks. But when your main story that you want an act break on wants to be two acts, you try to invent another act break. So we do think that way but I try not to impose it too early.

What are the classic problems?

Seriously? The story doesn't start before midway. We get too little information. Is it satisfying narratively and creatively? Are there surprises, do we have a second act complication – which often is the second commercial, if you're doing three acts... If you're in your second act of two acts and nothing new is happening, there's something wrong too. You want the whole thing to be cohesive, and there's a lot of ways how you may not end up having that. Then we discuss it as a group and kind of come to a consensus about what needs to change. We write everything down in the writers' room and everyone gets the same notes. We need to be our best critics. Because by the time the real critics come, which is the audience, it is too late to make changes. So we do the rewrite, and that usually takes another two to three days.

Is this done by the initial writer?

If we're in a quest for time, sometimes I might take scenes and just write them on my own, but they'd still get rewritten by the group.

You do the second draft in the room?

In a small group, yeah. You project it on the screen and you scroll through and if you're trying to fix a joke, you end up with a page and a half of possible jokes so you have to choose one, erase the others and put that one in. And that's usually 30–35 pages that you're rewriting. Then you take it to a table read. Often our table-read, schedule-wise, as we go to this time of the year, is one week before production. At the beginning we were doing two giant thorough rewrites, so we had the table read and the scenes got read by actors and then we went back to the room (again, he points to the dry erase board that has the outlined episode on it). For instance, here's a new scene, she goes from having a fight with Tracy to a scene with Jack that's supposed to motivate her to go back to Tracy and solve the problem with Jack's advice. But what was missing there was Jack wasn't giving specific advice, so what action was Liz taking to try to pursue her own agenda? Someone pitches out what that could be. And how that plays out differently.

And do these notes come from the actors?

I do talk with each of them after a table read. But, no, largely it's us. You're just hearing it.

And the actors know that what they are reading isn't there yet?

Yes, but they're great, they're giving us 100%. And that's very, very helpful. Because you cannot blame the performance, you can only blame the material. So now you're looking, if you're very lucky, at another three or four days of rewriting, again in a small group.

Do you do one episode after the other?

You're constantly doing several episodes at the same time. We start writing in June, start shooting in August, so at that point you're talking about two and a half months lead time. Right now Tina and I and another writer are writing our 100th episode, which is going to be an hour, which we've never done before. It's not even the end, we have another two episodes after it. So each of us three is writing their part and we are hopefully going to put that together over the weekend, so everyone can read and we have the actors next week; it's gonna be a little dicey. In other words now instead of two and a half months ahead we're about a week and a half ahead. So that's the platonic version of writing the show – the ideal, everyone's-happy-everyone's-included version. (laughs)

You're now in Season Five. How often have you experienced that version?

About half of the time, I'd say. 'Cause you have the two and a half months in the summer, and then it starts to be shorter. You got 22 episodes per season, so you shoot from August till the end of March. Usually you do four episodes and then you have a production hiatus so you have a little more writing time, then break over Christmas. If you do a show like we do with a single camera, like a movie, then the week off is a prep week for an episode. While at a multi-camera sitcom the week off is purely writing week, so we are two weeks ahead, because they need a published script to prep. And we got fortunately a very patient director who will get a script by the end of today and then he'll be prepping an hour and start shooting, I think a week from Monday. And he's got an outline, which is helpful. And then we're gonna read it hopefully on Wednesday in the hope that it works and we're gonna completely rewrite it through the weekend. So earlier in the year you are able to create more space before rewriting and shooting, at this time of year . . .

Do you ever have a real break?

When we finish shooting, end of March, Tina and I take a week vacation, we usually have three or four episodes to edit still, so that will take us all April and then we start again middle of June. So you get that month and a half to see your children.

That must be one of the hardest jobs there is?

We do take it very seriously that a lot of people are counting on this show. Tina tends to make the mistake of making quality part of the equation and it has gotten harder. Everything, comedy and drama, has to look like little movies and be much more intensive and more expensive. And the ratings are important. Yeah, having done movie work – nothing that has ever been produced but at least I've been paid for it – it's much worse in one way but the great thing is you have control. We have the final say. It's a responsibility we wouldn't want to give to someone else.

But the deadline pressure is immense . . .

I do find that if you have four people in the room, everyone is focusing and contributing. At six and seven, two people break out. Pressure can be good, you know. It can make you see things you wouldn't if you had too long to think about it. But you also see things you should have done better, you know, the shower principle . . .

Do you even get to have these moments? The space which allows you to have ideas out of the blue?

Sometimes. Often, we will be here until five in the morning. If I have the choice, I prefer to call it an early night and be here early – sometimes three morning hours will be more productive than an allnighter. But you don't always have that choice. I think it makes a big difference if you do.

Did Friends *work in the same way?*

It was different because production was so different. At *Friends* we shot on Friday night. It took about five or six hours to shoot the whole thing. In front of an audience. At *Raymond* they would do the whole thing in three hours, the whole half hour. But you're spending the rest of that week rewriting and rehearsing, which sometimes…You know, it is funny on Monday but it is not funny anymore on Thursday, because we've become tired of it, the actors have become tired of it, it becomes an old thing…But also every night you're rewriting based on the rehearsal you've seen, you're getting more information. So we were ahead of our game, we could consciously say, this is the thing that is really in trouble, and take a light pass on the rest. So the room out of necessity would run differently. Every night there would be a late night room. The basic process is still the same. There is just the distinction between multi-camera and single-camera. I think when (David) Mamet was doing a TV show, a military action show, he said, as he was getting into production, that "doing a movie is like running a marathon, doing a TV show is like running until you die." (laughs)

Good line!

Yeah, I heard it in an interview in relation to that show. You get onto a treadmill and it does not stop. And you're going fast. It helps when the show is a good one. I've been on shows that were considered bad, and I was still trying my hardest.

Do you always do a final polish?

We do the room polishing and I'm leading that. So if there's four jokes under consideration, we'll have our group discussion and I will make a decision – this is all preceded by Tina and I having a discussion about it. What I send to her is as close to what I think is the final version. So when she sends her notes back, I try to incorporate these into my own.

Do you ever think that if there were more time you could do all this without a room, that you could just write the whole thing?

You know, we certainly couldn't do the number of episodes we do in the time we have. I also don't think they'd be as good. If we have an average of three stories an episode, we're doing almost 70 stories a year. With a beginning, middle and end, for a variety of different characters. But I guess when it works, it is a combination of individual work and collaborative work – I mean, every genius author has a great editor! The collaborative thing is important but beyond that, at the end of the day, it feels like it's Tina's voice. I'm taking a lot of pride in having led that effort, but you're only benefiting from it if you have a good room. I've been in rooms that were very carefully put together, and they didn't work...

So how do you put a room together?

You read material, you meet people, often you hire people you've worked with before. And you try to find a blend of skills. Specially if there are a lot of different characters to write. Tracy is a poor African-American, so very different from Liz's middle-class Philadelphia college-educated background.

So you get someone for each character?

Not really. Setting aside Tracy as a specific case – if someone has a similar background like Tracy, it's great – what you want is people who can write everybody. Diversity is what you're looking for. We've had writers who didn't go to college. Writers who grew up as Jehovah's Witness. We have stand-ups who want that other life after driving around the country and chasing stand-up gigs. We have a bunch of Harvard nerds. We have so many people, and some things will help with certain characters, and some not. In terms of the creative process I like seeing experiences from different people, different approaches to creativity, and you want to sit down with different people.

Do you keep the room as it is throughout the whole series?

Ideally you want to have a room that stays. Last year we had a lot of turnover.

Would you do a cop show?

I'd love to do a cop show.

Would you get the chance to do a cop show?

That's what I like about this show. I think it is hard to say that a writer coming from this show can't do anything. I think *30 Rock* is an excellent training ground and I see my role as showrunner as, in large, educating and training the writers under me.

Do you also encourage them to take risks? You do get the feeling that you take risks around here.

Well, Tina is a person who wants to take risks.

One last question. Do you like your writing?

Sometimes. I'm often embarrassed by my writing, but I'm also capable of being proud of it at times. And in TV there's a certain point where you have to turn it in, whatever you think of it. (laughs) So that helps.

Janet Leahy

Janet Leahy's television credits include *The Cosby Show*, *Cheers*, *Roseanne*, *Boston Legal* and *Gilmore Girls*. Most recently she has worked on the AMC drama series *Mad Men*. She has won two Emmys and a WGA award.

So how did you become a TV writer?

I went to UCLA and received a nice award from The Hollywood Radio and Television Society. This eventually landed me a job as a secretary at the sitcom *Newhart*. It was there that I first learned the basics of good storytelling, taking notes in a room filled with funny, talented writers. Like everyone, I tried writing a script, and it was pretty mediocre, but the second was better, the show bought it and I decided maybe I could be a writer.

What did you study at UCLA?

I was a production major in the School of Film and Television. I definitely did not have plans to become a screenwriter. I was hoping to be a director and producer, but I knew I needed to learn how to tell stories. Writing those first scripts was more like giving something a shot, and if it didn't work out, it didn't work out. It wasn't entirely planned.

Janet, you have written for three of the very few shows that people know all over the world and that are still being broadcast all over the world: Cheers, The Cosby Show *and* Roseanne. *You must be a very rich woman.*

(laughs) Well, I'll tell you what is very interesting. You receive residual checks, and *The Cosby Show*'s residual checks should have run out a long time ago in a natural progression of things … but of all of the residual checks I am receiving, *The Cosby Show* shows up the most. *Roseanne* and *Cheers* also show up. But you'd be shocked how residuals just keep coming in for *The Cosby Show*. We must have hit something very universal.

You certainly did. I travel a lot, and whenever I turn on the TV in some hotel in some country, there's always either The Cosby Show *or* Cheers *or* Roseanne. *These series feel like home.*

(laughs) I'm very lucky in that sense.

And then you even went on to write for one of the freshest shows ever on TV, Boston Legal. *It seems like you guys had almost no boundaries – especially regarding political correctness issues. Is that true?*

Again I was very lucky. My boss and creator of the show, David E. Kelley[1] allowed me to take the reins and write whatever I wanted. Plus, because

David had so much clout, and therefore a great deal of leeway in what he was able to produce, I worked freely under his umbrella. The staff and I had to take care of the legal aspects. We followed the same guidelines as investigative journalists, citing our sources. And we ran everything by our legal department. But, as long as we covered our bases we could do whatever we wanted, and I was really proud of the show in that sense. It ran at a time where there was an imbalance of power in the government and media, and the show provided a space for more than one voice.

When you referred to Obama and Hillary Clinton, that was at a time when the country was in the midst of elections, right? Didn't the show influence people in terms of how they would vote?

I'm not sure about that. I was proud, though, of what we did do. The staff and I were curious about a lot of things and we had unbelievable researchers, so we would send them off researching, and the result was original material. Occasionally it worked out that our show – which took six to eight weeks to produce – would air nearly the same day as a major story was published in the newspaper. So *Boston Legal* would appear much fresher than other television shows.

You must have had a few angry letters from upset politicians or lobbyists?

We did get angry letters, but more often than not we got a huge number of letters in support. We received letters from teachers, doctors, mothers, people whose voice wasn't often heard. (laughs) Actually, we were President Clinton's favorite show at the time, that's what he told Oprah.

For me, as a European, it seemed more like a debate – whatever issue you were dealing with, you were actually able to hear both sides of it, or more.

But the thing is that, like in *The Cosby Show* – I learned a lot of things at *The Cosby Show* – you can't have that debate unless you're entertaining your audience. I'm an expert, hopefully, in entertaining people, and that's where the comedy would come in. It allowed us to play with the drama and create a roller coaster ride. Because just at the moment where it looks like you're going to preach to people, or take yourself too seriously, you cut out of there with something funny. And just like in life, you could be laughing one moment and suddenly things take a dark turn. The brilliant actors could pull that off. So, to me, your number one job at all times is to entertain people, and the fact that you can have your opinion heard is just good fortune.

Did you have a writers' room?

Yes, though writers' rooms work differently on different shows. I came from half-hour comedy television so I ran the room more along those lines. We also had a diverse group of writers with different skill sets. There were those who were better at drama, writers better at comedy, legal experts (lawyers who became writers), some gifted with story. Given that set of circumstances, I used our resources strategically. Each show usually contained three stories, so we broke each story individually and then matched them up, balancing the tone of drama with comedy. We'd create the first story on the boards, I'd pass out scenes to each writer. We'd bring it together, I would do a rewrite, then we'd move on to the next story. When all three stories were finished, I would work with another writer and weave them together.

So you wouldn't give the whole script to one writer.

No, though that is the case on most television shows, it wouldn't have been effective here. There was a time factor involved, as well as the best use of the skills we each possessed. It was a specific strategy to get over those hurdles. I did the rewrites in order to have one singular voice. You'll see the same thing in a show like *Mad Men*. That voice is Matthew Weiner's voice.

What about the studio? When did they get to see a draft?

We rarely received notes from the studio or network because of David's clout. Our draft would go up to David, he would call with his notes. The other executive producer, Bill D'Elia, gave his notes and we'd do our rewrites. Occasionally the network called with a note, but it couldn't be more than three or four times. We had a lot of freedom to do what we wanted. (laughs) In order to have that freedom you have to do an excellent job.

And I guess it also helps to be David Kelley?

(laughs) Actually, I was lucky because on *The Cosby Show* it was the same way. *Roseanne* and *Cheers* also had very little studio or network input.

How much did the actors contribute in Boston Legal? *Or in* The Cosby Show? *Or* Roseanne?

Those three particular shows you just singled out, the lead actors did have a voice – and I'll be specific. At *Boston Legal* David E. Kelley had promised James (Spader) that he could have input into his character, which is very rare. So I worked very closely with James on his material – we spent many a weekend discussing his closing argument, as he had one almost every week. In terms of *The Cosby Show* – well, that show was Bill's show and he would have a great deal of input. After each table read Bill would give his thoughts, and we'd base any rewrites on those thoughts, as well as our own notes from what we heard. At the time, comedies were videotaped or filmed in front of an audience. On *The Cosby Show* the first audience would come in the afternoon, and we shot it like a play, moving the cameras to each set, for each scene in the progression. Then a second audience would come in the evening and we would shoot the show a second time. So we would have two performances. And Bill would do the script as written in the afternoon, and then the evening show was his. I've never ever worked on a show like that before.

Or after.

Or after. And Bill is a master of improv, so he would sometimes just take off on a riff during an evening show. And you didn't know where he was going, and it was the job of Phylicia (Rashad) or whoever he was playing with – typically he would do it with Phylicia or Malcom Jamal Warner – to draw him with an unscripted line back into the show, and the script. That was something really wonderful to behold, to see where he could go with this. Then we would edit the two shows together. That was incredibly different from any show I had worked on before or after. *Roseanne* I worked on in the later seasons. When I was there Roseanne had input in the story stage, approving the stories. She had a very strong sense of truthfulness. And if it wasn't honest, you heard about it and if it wasn't funny you heard about it too. She hired a lot of stand-ups from her days on the road, and that was a great pool of talent. We had whole books of back-up jokes, alternatives for every line, I mean large books ... Again, it's all about making it great.

What about the writers' rooms there and a typical week?

Oh yeah, sitcoms, of course. I will give you the description of a typical week. On Monday, you would have a table read, in the morning. Based on what you heard, you worked on the rewrite that afternoon and evening. Tuesday morning the writers would work on the next week's script or pitch out a future episode. A writer would then take that story, go away and write. In the afternoon on Tuesday you went to the stage to see a run-through in which the actors performed the script for the writers and producers. Tuesday night would be big rewrite night – depending on the show, that could go into the wee hours of the morning. Wednesday morning you would be working on future scripts and in the afternoon there was a run-through of the current episode with the studio and network. Again, there would be a rewrite based on what you saw. Thursday would be for camera blocking. The cameras were brought in, the actors would find their specific marks on stage and they would rehearse with the director. Friday afternoon there would be a dress rehearsal, if it was film. And if it was videotaped, there would be an audience and you would actually shoot it. The second show would be shot that night. In between all that you were pitching more new stories and doing rewrites on existing scripts.

So basically you're in boot camp, and you can't have a life during that time.

You have friends and family who hopefully understand, and occasionally get ornery (laughs). It's very difficult in production. But you had the spring off, usually March, April and some of May.

Did you use improv on Boston Legal *as well? Sometimes it sounds like you did.*

No, never. It was all scripted. The only show that was improvised was *Cosby*. It's unheard of. That show was unusual in many, many respects.

You also wrote for Gilmore Girls, *and there you had the case of a discontinued showrunner.*

Yes, Amy Sherman Palladino, who created the show. But she ran that show for almost its entire run.

Does this happen often?

Oh yeah. That's not unusual at all. It's a hard job.

How important is the concept of the writers' room, do you think, for American TV's global success?

I think it's everything. As far as I can tell, no one person has come up with all the stories for a season of television. That's a fallacy. A writers' room is critical. Not just for the individual stories each writer brings in, but because the explosion of story telling that goes on back and forth as the result of bringing these people together. It really is extraordinary.

When you write a movie, you write alone. On TV it is many minds in one room. Does it all add up or is there a danger that it takes away from the truth?

Oh it can, absolutely. And that can happen if the show runner doesn't have a strong sense of story telling, or panics under the stress and settles for something less than excellent. The best showrunners are those with a strong voice for the truth, originality and entertainment. And the writers' rooms are dictatorships. This is important, in order to hear that voice. Television is a team sport, and you have to follow the vision of the creator and that's hard for people at times. The goal is to put out a great show, and whatever you have to do to get there, you do. The best TV writers know they're part of a team; the most difficult ones are those who don't understand the team concept and they generally don't last long.

So how can you become a showrunner? How do you do the training at the Showrunner Training Program?

The program running at the Writers Guild, and you can apply to it as a TV writer, meets every Saturday for several months. Reputable showrunners come in and pass on their knowledge. Studio executives and other industry professionals also come in and share their experience. It's a very successful program; a lot of people who have come out of there run shows now.

You also worked on Life Unexpected, *a show which got canceled after its second season. That does happen a lot nowadays...*

Yes, it does. On that show Liz Tigelar created a wonderful pilot, but had never run a show before. They asked me to come in and run the show with her. She's a very talented writer and incredibly well organized, talented producer. So my biggest contribution was in keeping the storytelling on track. My goal was to get the show launched and a second season pick-up. We did that. Unfortunately it was canceled some time during that second season. I was no longer with the show at the time, so I don't know what happened.

It looks like there are more men showrunners than women. How is it that women don't rise to the top?

They do. Just not as many as men. Traditionally, I think it's been because men like working with people they know and feel comfortable with, and that's usually other men.

So it's not that women don't have enough confidence to rise up the ladder?

No. There is just a lot of discrimination in this business. There's a great deal of age discrimination as well. I have a lot of friends who are out of work because they're over forty. But this business changes every day. And it's difficult for me to split things down gender lines, especially when I see so many successful women out there creating shows every day. Opportunities are shifting constantly. The platforms are shifting. How we receive our stories changes all the time. I guess my point is that one can look at these things with discouragement, or one can create their own opportunities.

What are you up to these days?

The past few years I've been over at *Mad Men*. I consulted over there for two years, and this year I'm working full time as an executive producer.

Can you tell us any secrets about the season?

(laughs) Never!

Eric Overmyer

Eric Overmyer joined the crew of *The Wire* as a consulting producer and writer in 2006 – that was the show's fourth season. He had previously worked on *St. Elsewhere, Homicide: Life on the Street* and *Law & Order*. Together with David Simon he then co-created the HBO drama *Treme*. He has won a WGA award and an Edgar.

Why do you think that American TV showcases better writing than American movies?

A lot of American television is just as bad as American cinema. It's just cable that provides that environment where you can make different stuff.

Do you always work with writers' rooms?

We convene our writing staff on *Treme* – and it was the same with *The Wire* – three weeks before we start writing the scripts for the upcoming season. We don't have a daily – I mean, some other shows meet daily, which I never understood, because how you're gonna write if you meet daily? You talk and talk and talk, and it's boring, so I'm not a fan of that. Actually we had a really wonderful writers' room, and we met a couple of times between the pilot and the start of the shooting and once or twice as well during the season. But, for instance, when we were shooting Episode Eight, David (Simon)[1] was rewriting the next one, and David and George (Pelecanos)[2] and I would meet and talk out the last three episodes of the season. That's our kind of writers' room.

What do you do when you meet? Do you just brainstorm or do you actually break the story together?

David and I, and one or two other people perhaps, we come to a consensus of what the story should be about. Sometimes David and I will do the first draft, but often it is an outside writer. A freelance writer. They're not genuinely outside writers, they've been included in the process all along.

Do you actually ever use terminology like acts, turning points etc.?

In our case we don't have to have acts. We do a teaser, but that's all. It's very nice to not have acts.

How do you organize the story?

We organize the scripts, yes. But, you know, in *Treme*, because the show is about music, and some of the characters are actual musicians, and we shoot all the music live, we figure it out on the spot. They are not playing to playback, so there's good energy but it's also tricky when to go into a song and when to get out of it. It's a very interesting element to be working with. And it's a real joy, it's a great pleasure.

You can feel the joy, when you watch it...What about The Wire? *I read somewhere that you were credited with the domestic stories.*

It's not true! There were a few occasions where David said, "Would you please write that scene?" – he didn't want to write the scenes between the character and his wife. We were joking about it. And I was only there for one season, the fourth season. When they started I was busy with *Law and Order*, where I was on staff for five seasons. And when I left *Law and Order*, David asked me whether I would like to come in. And when the season was over, because HBO had a very long schedule, I couldn't wait for the fifth season of *The Wire*, so I took another job.

Don't you ever dry out of ideas, when you're on a show for too long?

I suppose you could. I worked on *Homicide* for three years and, generally speaking, if the situation's good, you want to stay.

Where did you learn writing for TV?

I knew Tom Fontana...

Of course.

(laughs) Yes. I knew him from the theater in New York, and then he became a very powerful writer-producer, so he called me and asked whether I would like to write a script, and I said yes. There are certain things which are similar to theater, character and dialogue work, but everything else is different: the fact that you have to write characters that have been created by someone else, and you have to execute it properly, in the house style, so to say. There's a certain amount of ego involved there. It's a question of whose intellectual property it is. When you're on staff on a television show you want to bring something to it and you want to make it better, but it doesn't belong to you. Theater and TV are very different forms, there's no question.

Don't you miss the theater?

It depends on my situation in television. Right now I am pretty happy. I had an attachment to New Orleans for a very long time. We have a house here but my family is in New York, so I live in New York. I have also been frustrated in television, it can be exhausting – but writing for the theater has its challenges as well.

What about working with Pelecanos? Him being a novelist, don't you have a different creative process?

He has done a lot of television, though. If you'd talk with him you'll find out that he'd much rather be writing his new novel than anything else, but I think he enjoys writing for us.

I've heard two prevailing opinions concerning rewriting. The majority says that they have to rewrite to give the series a unique voice and there's another one, which says I want to keep the individual voice of each writer in the show.

David and I both wish we were the second case... I do think some showrunners are complete control freaks and rewrite everything. But this show doesn't have a staff, it's David and me. If I have a staff, it actually makes me angry when I get a script I need to rewrite, because these people get a lot of money, and if I have to spend my Saturday rewriting someone else's script, I'm not happy. On this show we don't expect the writers to get it as well as we do, it's a very tricky show, but we do want them to do something different with the characters, that they go to places we haven't gone to, that they have a new angle on something. And that some of their distinctive voice comes out. So we hope for the latter and we end up more often than not with the former. What you want is someone to catch the voice of the show but from their own fresh perspective. And we want to have to make the most minimal polish necessary to get that draft done for production.

Sometimes it's about having a different taste, don't you think?

It's about advancing the story and capturing the essence of the characters. There's some shows like *The West Wing*, where all characters have to talk in a very certain way, all the same, that banter... And people who like that show, that's important to them, they want them to sound the same. You know, everyone's bright, and that's appropriate for that show. If other shows had that, they would be weak shows. In that case they were really writing for one character.

Do you ever get the feeling that something gets destroyed in development?

Oh sure. Network executives want everything explained, they want to simplify everything, and you often get that feeling that the draft gets weaker and weaker. That's commonplace. That is not the same with HBO. They have more questions, they try to understand what's happening there; it is a creative approach.

It sounds like paradise.

They do come from a different place. In a way, it was MTM's philosophy too, you know: hire good writers and get out of their way. Which sounds logical, but most TV executives don't do that. HBO does, they are of a similar philosophy. They believe in this project and they trust David and me to do our work. Studios are dealing by fear, they're afraid of sponsors, they anticipate, and make sure that disasters don't happen. There's a lot of people whose job is to give notes. You get endless notes, making it more palatable, less spicy, more melodramatic, more like what has been done before.

That has been my experience as a TV writer in Europe. I always thought that that is what makes the whole difference creatively, whether you are operating from fear or not – and that in American TV there is more creative freedom. You are destroying my illusion.

(laughs) But that's the majority here as well. It's only as you say for a handful of shows – HBO and Showtime and FX, maybe AMC. That's a very few programs in the vast wasteland of American television.

So you don't ever get notes from HBO?

They see the first published draft, which goes to production crew. And then, if there are any notes, we'll do blue pages.

So they get to see it together with the production departments? They are not involved in the stage where you're talking story?

Before the scripts are written there's a point where David will call a couple of executives, and they will talk in very general terms.

So you basically have the final word and the final cut.

We take HBO notes seriously. Some we can do, some we can't. We're happy to do, if it doesn't bother us or if we agree with it. If it's a good idea. Otherwise we will say no and explain why. There are very few occasions where they will insist. If they insist…well, it's their show, they own it. But it never comes to that.

Are there any unspoken don'ts?

Don't be stupid? (laughs) No, there's nothing which is not allowed. Perhaps a racist or sexist remark which does not come out of character. But that we wouldn't want either.

Are writers typecast?

For sure. You write police or medical.

Don't you ever want to do comedy?

Yeah. That's the hardest one. If you want to get from drama to comedy or comedy to drama. It would be a huge career switch.

What about writing for movies?

It's jealously guarded by the A-list writers who get a lot of money to do rewrites. I'd love to get some of that work too. It's hard to get. If I had more time I'd write a spec script.

Where do you get time to live?

There was a writers' strike a few years ago.

That strike saved your lives then, did it? Sometimes, it sounds like you guys are imprisoned for months in a row.

It's true, but it is satisfying too, so it doesn't feel like prison. Last year I had a break on *Treme*, and I did *In Treatment*, so that was interesting... But you want to keep writing. I had some dry patches, and that's no fun.

Do you have projects on the side?

I have a couple of notions. But you don't pitch them at the same time you're on a show. You're not allowed to work for anyone else contractually. I guess theoretically I could go pitch something to HBO but they will look at me and say, aren't you supposed to be working on *Treme*? They would be suspicious that I wasn't kind of keeping my eye on the ball.

And when you finish, you magically pull these five projects out of your bag.

(laughs) Exactly.

American TV rooms seem to mainly consist of white men who live in L.A. That's a very small percentage of the population.

There are more women than you realize – but they also tend to be white. I don't know. I don't think there's many good TV writers, I think most writers on television are appallingly mediocre. You've got a dozen or so who are really good writers, but there are a lot of writers who go from show to show because they got credits and they turn in a script and get rewritten by the showrunner and they never advance in their skills. The studio knows them, they got a resume that keeps getting longer but their work never actually gets done – their script is rewritten, they don't do any real producing and it's very hard. It's a very odd, kind of discouraging system. If I were to start a show and I were allowed to hire a big staff, I might be able to come up with ten names – and they're all people I've worked with before. It's because I don't know other people. And because it's very risky taking a chance on somebody you don't know. It's a very closed system.

What about younger writers?

I've done this, especially with playwrights. The reality is you often inherit people and there's very few people you can hire, and you also have to get everybody approved. Once you're in, you do well. Everybody is looking for a decent writer who is black and a woman. But it's hard to get in – and it's harder and harder these days. It's like musical chairs, where the chairs get fewer and they keep sending people in.

The film schools keep sending people in.

Yes. Plus the staffs get smaller. The studios are owned by shareholders, they look at the balance, they are not studios any more.

Do you choose the directors?

They have to be found by HBO. That's a big thing to get through, for a director. It's always a gamble to work with someone you don't know. Like with the writers. There are a lot of filmmakers who would like to do the show, but they're not big enough for HBO to approve them.

So they are more strict concerning the names attached than with the content?

They are worried about lack of experience in doing this. We do an 11-day shoot, it is much more high-pressure than a feature, and in our show we have the additional challenge of music and the parades. Ok, you've done some independent features but you've never done an HBO show. You don't have the experience. But how do I get that experience, if you don't hire me? That's a tough one. I don't know. I don't make these decisions. The line producer and HBO hire the directors. They ask me if I have an objection, but she works that out with the HBO executives, and she does those calls and she looks at a lot of material.

Is there anything I overlooked you would like to talk about?

Oh gosh, no, I don't think so. You know what you're talking about, being in the business yourself.

Ok then, I have a last one: are you at this much coveted point in your career where you can get made whatever you want?

No, not at all! I can get in and pitch, but whether it gets made, that's a whole different story. I may even have trouble making my next show. There are so many factors . . . it's like lightning in a bottle.

Jane Espenson

Jane Espenson's television credits include *Buffy the Vampire Slayer*, *Battlestar Galactica*, *Game of Thrones*, *Torchwood*, *Once Upon a Time* and the original series *Husbands*, created with Brad Bell. She has won two Hugo awards.

Why do you think that American TV has so much better writing right now than most American movies?

TV in general is a writer's medium. You get to dictate the stories, produce your own material, be on set, and whatever else ... supervise the editing ... Even a low-level TV writer has arguably more control over the final product than a much more experienced feature writer. I think there are some gorgeously written movies out there, but, yeah, TV has so much to offer that I'm not surprised that a lot of the most creative voices work here.

Where did you learn to write and when did you feel comfortable enough to start answering the question "and what do you do" with "I'm a writer"?

I don't think you need anything to learn to write other than to watch and to think critically about what you're seeing. It's like learning to build a machine – the best education comes from studying other machines and learning to extrapolate the general principles of mechanics from them. Not by learning the principles and then setting out to invent something from them. For one thing, that's just too hard. So I started learning to write TV when I was a kid, watching episodes of *Barney Miller* or *Soap* or *MASH* or *Welcome Back, Kotter* and thinking about what made them work. I thought a lot about character and dialogue and jokes – in retrospect I should've looked at structure, too, but what I got worked well enough. I didn't study writing in college other than a few courses, none of them on TV writing – UC Berkeley didn't really offer anything relevant at the time. I guess I was forced to pick it up on the streets. The question about saying "I'm a writer" – that's funny you ask that. I used to think of that all the time – looking forward to saying that. I said it when I got my first staff job in TV – on the show *Dinosaurs*. I loved saying it – I still do. It's still thrilling. Who gets to make their living by means of the funnest hobby ever?! It's like being a paid "thinker." I remember I even enjoyed writing it on the unemployment forms during a year I didn't get staffed on a show.

You are also a scholar, how does one influence the other?

Ha! "Scholar" sounds very, sort of, a couple centuries ago. But I like it. It's more like I was one of those perpetual students, until I found a way to flop out of the nest. I was studying metaphor, which has turned out to be very important for what I do – especially when I'm writing on a science fiction show. Sci-fi is mostly about metaphor. But I can't say that anything I studied has really affected stories I've written. It's more like what I studied and what I write are just both products of the same general way of wanting to make generalizations about the world. I like to abstract things.

You are one of the very few writers who are very far from ever being pigeon-holed, as you seem to be able to write comedy and drama and science fiction too. How did you ever manage that? Moreover, you seem different than most writers in that you do not seem to like to stay on one and the same show for a very long time; you seem to like the variety of different genres and stories. How come?

I think you'll find most TV writers are out of work every single year just because that's how the stats shake out. Most shows are canceled. I would've loved to have settled in for longer tenures at lots of the shows I've written on. Truth is, I think *Gilmore Girls* and *The OC* may have been the only shows I've written on that continued after I left, and *The OC* was always meant to be a temp job. Eureka – I was there very briefly... The other shows all ended their runs while I was there, forcing me to move on. Counting idly, I just came up with 11 shows I've worked on that ended while I was there. And I think I missed a couple. Maybe I ran them into the ground! But this hasn't been a bad thing for me – bad for the shows, though, and some, like *Firefly*, deserved far longer runs. But personally, I love a buffet – lots of different bites and I'm glad my career has been like that. The transition from comedy shows to dramas was thoughtful – I realized it was a better fit. The rest was happenstance – I was offered *The OC* and *Gilmore* both right after *Buffy*, and I guess that helped make me palatable to non-sci-fi shows. My comedy background made me a good fit for shows like *Jake in Progress* and *Andy Barker, PI*, so I was able to slip back and do a little more comedy. And my agent knows that I like moving around, so he doesn't hesitate to bring me other options – animated or whatever. If there were still jobs in soaps, I'd totally want to try that, too, since that's something I've never done.

You have been around quite a long time. Do you think things have changed or are changing on TV? Are more things possible? Do you really get to experiment as much as it looks like from the outside, and have the freedom one feels you have from the outside?

God, I have been around a long time. 19 years. I can't believe it! I still feel like a new kid so much of the time. Things have changed in various ways: much more diversity in the writers' room. Less money – the huge "deals" went away. More shows, more kinds of shows – something like *Spartacus*, or *Torchwood*, or *Mad Men*, or *Community* – they would've been too "niche" when I started. Smaller writing staffs. More internet content. Yeah, there are huge opportunities to experiment, but it is still providing a product to a corporate entity that has certain hopes and expectations. It's not all that free. But the kinds of products you can offer them … that's where it's gotten freer.

Did all the shows you have worked on have writers' rooms? Which was the one that worked best for you and for the show?

Rooms are different for every show. But so far they've all had them. Some shows don't – each writer works one-on-one with the showrunner on their episodes. But I've always worked on shows where at the very least we have a period at the beginning of each major arc where we all sit together to plot out the story. That process is usually pretty similar everywhere – the showrunner comes in with a general road map and we all throw in ideas for landmarks along the way. After that, things diverge a lot. In comedy rooms, the room is used to actually rewrite the scripts as a team. In dramas, it's usually used to provide ideas and structure for upcoming episodes. We "break" the episodes. Sometimes it's writers around a table, sometimes it's writers draped across sofas. It can be loud and disorganized and drifty, or quiet and focused. You can use a monitor or a corkboard or a whiteboard. It's all very … varied.

You joined Caprica *as a showrunner during the first season. How did that work for you?*

It was interesting. I wasn't clear on what the hard parts were going to be, but I knew it was going to be hard. And it was even harder than that. I don't think I excelled – I wasn't prepared to deal with all the demands. And I didn't like that I no longer had time to really sink into the single-minded writing of an episode. I ran back to that role when I had the chance. If I create a show in the future, I'm going to have to figure out a way to preserve that.

Cable had started as the place where you did not need ratings, because there is no advertising. Now ratings are suddenly important – people like to cite Caprica *as the one example which made that clear.*

Hmm … That's interesting. But I don't know enough about the business models and haven't bothered to educate myself. Point me at a script and I'll write it. I don't actually worry about much beyond that.

I have not been able to watch much of Caprica *but what I watched I found utterly fascinating and very actual. It was as if it were talking about us today, and about the world before the crisis, showing what led us to the present crisis. But then SyFy canceled the show, before it had a chance to catch the audience's attention. That did seem quite impatient – and a waste?*

The ratings weren't high because people weren't watching. In retrospect, I can point to things I suspect we did wrong, things I did wrong, in building suspense and capturing a broad audience's attention. But I'm sure even hit shows can point to missteps – it's not clear how helpful that is after the fact. I'd like to think the premise had the potential to be a big hit, but it didn't draw the eyeballs. I assume SyFy has a way to project what the ceiling is going to be on a show once it has some basic data – they must have had reason to think it was never going to reach enough people to make it make financial sense. It is a shame, but I have amazing hopes for *Blood and Chrome*, the new Battlestar prequel they're doing now with my good friend Michael Taylor.

When you communicate with other writers, like in the writers' room, do you use terms like acts, turning points, climax?

Sure! Of course! Acts, act breaks, story turns, character moments, A-story, B-story, reveals … probably any term you've read in a "how to write for TV" book … we use all those terms. They're the names for the parts of the machines that we make.

Where did you learn to run a show?

Ha! I didn't! I always just wanted to write. So when I worked for great showrunners like Joss Whedon and Ron Moore and now Russell Davies, I tended to watch how they craft characters and dialogue and scenes … not how they ran the show! I would've run *Caprica* better if I'd learned. The Writers Guild has a showrunning class, but I didn't take it, since I didn't expect to run a show.

Will you walk me through the development of one episode of Caprica, *for instance? Did you define the core story on your own and then take it to the writers' room?*

We were very lucky to have Ron Moore involved in *Caprica*. He took us, the writing staff, on a writers' retreat in which he laid out, with our help, the arc for 10 or 11 episodes. At that point the general notion behind each episode was determined. When we were back in the room, the staff and I would take that idea and talk it over in a big group to try to find some structure inside the basic beginning-middle-end plus theme. Once we had that, we'd get more specific, determining scenes. Then we pitched it to Ron and would get more input... finally a specific writer would be sent out to write the episode.

Whose decision is it to which writer to assign which episode?

The showrunner can assign them, but usually the writers have essentially already assigned themselves by demonstrating an affection for one episode or another. On some shows it cycles around in a set order, but even then, a writer may go out of order if they are particularly attached to an episode. Often this happens because it's an idea they brought to the room.

I have heard two prevailing opinions during interviews. One is of the majority, which says that the showrunner has to polish or even rewrite all scripts to give the series a single voice. Then there are the showrunners who want to keep the distinctive voices in each episode, even see a different side of the characters accentuated depending on the writer, and who only do rewriting when absolutely necessary. What do you think – as a writer and as a showrunner?

I understand both ways of thinking. I actually think it depends on the show. I think *Gilmore Girls* benefited from the very specific voice that Amy Sherman-Palladino could bring. I think *Battlestar Galactica* benefited from the way episodes sometimes had clear and different authorial styles. I'll say that even the most let-the-writers-be-different shows still have some showrunner rewriting, though. As a writer, I like to hear my words. As a showrunner, I like to hear my words. So I probably rewrite a little more as a showrunner than writer-me would like. Oh well.

How is that different for a writer (to be rewritten by a showrunner) than what she experiences in the movies, when a director will easily rewrite a script to make it their own? And what is it for you, this need for rewriting? Is it about having a different taste from the original writer? I guess you have been rewritten as well.

A director may "readily" rewrite a script, but I don't know if they do it "easily." Rewriting is hard. Sometimes it's harder than writing because first you have to erase what you just read. It's often harder to preserve pieces of the original than it is just to start over. There are so many kinds of rewriting and so many reasons to do it that it's hard to talk about as a single thing. Every writer rewrites their own material several times before they turn it in. Then they get notes from the showrunner, then from the studio and the network. Then the showrunner takes their pass. Then production changes necessitate more changes. Then a scene is lost in editing so the line has to be changed again to cover some lost exposition and the actor is brought in to record it and lay it in over the finished scene. It's amazing that any lines get through from first draft to screen. The most common reason to rewrite probably has to do with adjusting a scene in some overall way – changing what happens or the point of view or the characters' take on it. But sometimes it's about the voice of a character or the rhythm of a joke. Lots of times, the showrunner just had something different in mind. Showrunners have all been writers and they've been rewritten dozens of times. It's not a bad or hurtful thing. The show isn't there to give the writers a chance to hear their words. The writers are there to serve the show and the showrunner. The showrunner has a big-picture perspective and it is their vision. When I look at a scene that Russell or Ron or Joss has rewritten, I usually end up making mmm noises at how beautiful it turned out.

I believe there are also two different ways to go regarding credits. Showrunners who get credited almost for every script, others who don't and consider their rewriting part of being a showrunner. Which one do you find more fair – as a writer or as a showrunner?

It's pretty much an accepted thing in TV that the original writer retains the credit. That rewriting is, as you say, just part of being a showrunner. That's the way I usually see it done – that's how I do it. Some showrunners prefer credits that more accurately reflect the percentage of work they did. It's just a different way of looking at it. I wouldn't resent sharing credit with a showrunner that applied that system, I just happen to do it the other way.

American TV is selling all over the world with great success. Do you think about that world audience or any audience when you write?

I try not to take *any* audience into consideration. I've said this before, but I think you have to write what *you* want to watch. If you write for any other audience, you're aiming in the dark. If I trust that I have good taste, then what I like should automatically apply to others. Whether that also means it applies internationally ...? Well, I guess I don't see why it wouldn't.

There seems to be a trend towards foreign series being picked up for a remake.

Yes. My current show, *Torchwood*, has had three previous seasons as a UK show. I love the current climate that makes that possible.

Writing a series when in production leaves no time to breathe. Tell me what your year looks like. Is there time to live and experience new things to write about?

There's time to live, but not a lot of time to keep up to date on other TV shows – I hate that I'm too busy writing TV to watch it. This year is a great one, though. I'm loving my work on *Torchwood*, I'm also working on a couple pilots and some more *Buffy* comic book work. There's plenty to give me something to write every day from now until well into the summer. Actually, I think there is always something to write every day – it's hard to recall a time when I didn't have a pitch or outline or script due.

Do you remember living with the fear that what you deliver is not going to be good enough?

Yes, of course, I still have that fear. Writing is very subjective, and it wouldn't be unheard of for a writer of my experience to be told to start over, or to have a misfire of some kind. And until I get a complete "words on paper" draft, I'm always sure that this is going to be the time I simply don't get it finished. Having a finished script every time always surprises me – Hey! I did it!

As a staff writer on a TV show did you ever have the feeling that something was rewritten in the wrong direction?

Very rarely. I can think of only a couple examples – once on a sitcom, once on a drama, in which I felt that the rewrite was, let's say, lateral. Generally, things get better.

Did you have final word as a showrunner?

No, I did not – I was not the only executive producer on *Caprica*. But even if I were, there are still network executives and standard-and-practices people, and of course the production people who tell you what you can't afford ... I think it's way too collaborative for anyone to really feel they have final word.

Executives are like gatekeepers. You have to go through a gate guarded by a few people to get to the audience. Does this trouble you at all, does it change the way you write?

Hmm. It certainly changes the writing, since that's what they're there to do – ask you to change the writing when they feel it can benefit from their input. Usually this isn't such a bad thing. They've got a little more perspective, so they can see the story with fresher eyes. Does it trouble me? Not really – if I wanted to write only and exactly what I wanted, I could make my own web series. But if I want to use their system, that's the price I pay. I'm only troubled when I see something that looks like writers are being taken advantage of.

When do you stop changing the script?

On some shows, sometimes there are changes on the day something shoots. On sitcoms, they can change or add jokes between takes in front of an audience. And of course, material may be added and recorded during post-production. So, sort of, not until it airs.

Is there an evolution of formats? You have written webisodes – how different is that? What do you think is the future in terms of writing and the internet?

Writing webisodes is fun and different. The format seems to be settling into these stories in little bites, so you have to have a story turn every few pages. But then, as TV shows are adding more act breaks, that really isn't that unfamiliar. The thing I really like about webisodes is that they fit really well with one of my favorite things – taking a minor character and putting them center stage. In real life, no one is a supporting character – and in a well-written show, the same should be true. They're all stars who just haven't had their story told yet. I've always held that it's all gonna be one box – there won't really be a distinction between web series and TV series – and we'll all be scheduling our own viewing without a broadcast schedule. I actually thought this would all happen about ten years earlier. Does that make me a really good predictor or a really bad one?

Are there any unspoken don'ts in American TV?

Oh, I think they've all been pretty well spoken. Sometimes you hear a new one: don't set a show in college. Don't try to sell a period piece. Or whatever. And then someone does and it's a huge hit, so none of these really mean anything.

Writers' rooms seem to be full of white men and located in L.A. This seems like a very small percentage of the world population writing for the world population. I know why it started that way but I cannot really understand why it continues to be that way. Any insight?

Inertia, I suppose. Things tend to go on the same way until there's a really big counter-pressure making it impossible to continue. The rooms are actually a lot less white and male than when I started. They are still mostly in L.A., though, despite the fact that most shows now seem to shoot elsewhere. I guess we could all live all over the place and do it all with videoconferencing or something, but I think you'd lose something. The room is best when everyone is together.

Diana Son

Diana Son was most recently consulting producer for the NBC series *Do No Harm* and has been a writer/producer for the series *NYC-22*, *Blue Bloods*, *Southland*, *Law & Order: Criminal Intent* and *The West Wing*. She has also written pilots for CBS and A&E. She is the author of the plays *Stop Kiss*, *Satellites*, *BOY* and *R.A.W. ('Cause I'm a Woman)*.

It looks like American studios are now buying more and more formats for TV series from abroad.

Yes. Studios and networks are buying more and more foreign shows these days ... they're obsessed! (laughs) There's something about the idea of the show that they like but then they want you to make it yours. They want your "take" on it. And they give you a lot of freedom. One time I was sent a book by a producer about a young female lawyer in Washington D.C. who was Latina. They said "it doesn't have to take place in D.C., she doesn't have to be a lawyer and she doesn't have to be Latina." And I was like ... "OK ... so, then what is it about this book that you like?" (laughs) Another time I was given the DVD of a German series called "The Last Cop." In the German version, this cop had been in a coma for 20 years and woke up to find a changed world. So I did a little research and found out that basically anyone who was in a coma for even three months ... is not a viable person anymore. He cannot be a walking and talking person. But, I liked the idea of someone waking up to a changed world so I decided, OK, let's say he was in a coma for ten years. Still totally unrealistic but ... hey, it's TV (laughs) And there have been so many changes in the world in the last ten years – technology has changed, the politics of the New York Police Department has changed ... It ain't "Guiliani Time" anymore ... and his personal life would have changed. His adoring toddler daughter would be a sullen teenager now. I thought it could've been interesting without being too hokey. But the network ended up passing on it because they were already developing a pilot that had a similar premise.

Diana, you are one of the very few TV writers who are not located in Los Angeles. How do you manage?

It's hard. I definitely have fewer options. I mean, right now there are maybe three or four shows ... dramas, I mean, because I don't write comedy or talk shows ... that have their writing staffs in NYC. Meanwhile, there are over 100 in L.A., including shows on some of the smaller networks. But, you know, my life is here, I own my home, my kids are in school . . . So, whenever there's a new show in NYC I try to get hired on it. Sometimes it works out, sometimes it doesn't. So then, like with my most recent job, on *Do No Harm*, I have "commuted" to L.A. I was there every other week. But my showrunner was a great guy, a family man, so whenever I didn't *have* to be in L.A., like when I was writing my outline or script, then he let me stay in NYC. He'd say "Go home! Go be with your family." When I was on *Southland* I was in L.A. three days a week. It's tough on my family, obviously, I have a husband and three young kids. So, my goal is to run my own show based in NYC. I've written a few pilots but none have made it to series. But it's good to have goals! (laughs)

These were spec pilots?

No, not spec. Two of those pilots were based on ideas that the producer came to me with. The producers had sold the ideas to the networks and then I was brought on as a writer. But this past year, I sold a pilot that was based on an original idea. Every year each network buys around 100 pilots. And they'll choose to shoot anywhere from five to 11 of them. So, the odds are against you but you know, no one would be in this business if they worried about things like that! We all like to think "But oh, I will be the exception!" (laughs)

May I ask you what they will pay for a pilot?

Oh, man, that really ranges. I mean, if you're one of the name brand showrunners? Over a million dollars. But I think what is considered a premium pilot fee is around $150,000. You can get paid anywhere from the Writer's Guild minimum to $1 million plus depending on your experience.

And that is just for the writing of the script.

Right. That is just for the writing of the script. If they decide to shoot your pilot, then they pay you to produce it. An executive producer fee. Which, again, depending on the experience of the writer could vary wildly. $25,000 per episode for a novice writer, half a million dollars for a more experienced one. That fee will continue to be your executive producer fee if the pilot gets picked up to series. So, you would get that fee for every episode that was produced. So, for example, a typical season for a broadcast network show is 22 episodes. So, you would multiply that fee by 22. So, you see why so many starving playwrights end up writing for television! (laughs)

But someone on staff will get the Guild's minimum?

Well, it depends what you mean by being on staff. Any writer hired by a show is on its staff. But a "staff writer" is very specifically a first-year writer. It's an entry level position. And that person does get paid the Writer's Guild minimum, which is, I think, around $3500 a week? I think. But after that, once you move up a level and are a story editor, then most of the time you're getting paid above the Guild minimum. That's what your agent's for. Also, once you're a story editor then you start getting paid for your scripts. Around $35,000 for each one. So, the year you're a staff writer is really your "paying your dues" year. It gets you in the door. But you're not really paying off student loans or buying BMWs. You've got to stick with it a few years.

Still, this sounds like an awful lot of money.

It does *sound* like it (laughs). But only a handful of people are making crazy money. The rest of us are just trying to live middle class lives with our families. In very expensive cities. (laughs)

So a story editor is actually a writer, right?

Yes. It depends on the show – because every show is run differently – but in general, until you become a producer all you do is write and maybe produce your episode on set, but with an upper level writer/producer overseeing you. These titles, "story editor," "executive story editor," don't ... they're not a job description. It just means you're what's called a "lower level" writer. That sounds awful ... but I didn't make it up! Anyway, in my case it was not until I became a co-executive producer that I did more than just write my own scripts. And began rewriting other people's scripts, producing other writers' episodes on set, etc. But you know, I've been working in TV for over 14 years ... I've worked on six different shows and each one was run differently. It's all based on the preferences of your showrunner. On some shows, like *Law & Order: Criminal Intent*, the writing staff never met as a group. Never. Same thing on *NYC-22*. One of those showrunners said, "Sitting in a room with a bunch of writers all day is my idea of hell." And he was a nice guy! (laughs) Just being honest. But you know, writers are solitary people by nature. So, it's kind of ironic that so many shows have writers' rooms where writers sit around and pitch ideas out loud for eight–ten hours a day. It's not really the same skill as writing. It's related, but it's not the same.

So, what is your background? Where did you learn?

I'm a playwright.

You studied at NYU?

I was an undergrad at NYU. But I studied Dramatic Literature, I didn't study writing. My parents would never let me go to Arts School! It was bad enough I wasn't going to be a doctor. (laughs) So, for four years I read and analyzed plays and during my senior year I interned at La Mama, the experimental theater company in the East Village. After college, I did whatever I could...waitressing, teaching English as a Second Language, temping as a word processor, etc. Anything I could do that gave me enough flexibility that I could spend part of the day writing my plays. Then I had a play called *Stop Kiss* produced at the Public Theater that did very well and then I was able to go to Los Angeles and meet people in the film and TV world.

Was it the goal, to write for TV, or was it a compromise?

Well...(laughs) Theater is a more pleasurable experience.

You mean in the actual writing?

In a lot of ways. I mean, in the actual writing, yes, I am not trying to please anyone except me. Which is very liberating. While in TV writing you always have to think..."Will my boss like this?" or there'll be a time when I want to make a choice but I know my boss won't like it. You get caught up in second guessing. You're always trying to fulfill the aesthetic of the show and of your showrunner. When you're writing a play, you're writing in your own voice. You're not imitating anyone else. And the writing process itself is more engaging emotionally, you have to look into yourself. I always think that when you're writing a play you should be doing something that really scares you ...confronting something deep and personal. With TV...you know, you're writing on deadline, you have like eight–ten days to do a first draft so it's not really a spiritual experience! (laughs) If everyone likes it, the showrunner likes it, the producer likes it, the studio and network don't have a million notes...then you can feel like, wow, cool, I did a good job. And then your friends watch it on TV and they email you and say "I liked your episode." And that feels nice. But with a play, you know, it's like people come up to you afterwards, tears streaming down their face and they can't talk, "I don't know even what to say to you" – you know what I mean? It's a different kind of reward.

It's more about why you became a writer in the first place.

Yes.

So why do you write for TV?

The truth is, as a little girl growing up in a small town...I didn't go to plays. There was no theater! But I watched tons and tons of TV. So I do like writing for TV and it is in many ways a fulfillment of a dream. I would love to run my own show one day soon. But there's also the fact that in this country you cannot make a living as a playwright. It's impossible. You have to either teach full time, as in run a department, which doesn't leave you the time and energy to keep writing your own plays, or you have to write for TV or film. But don't get me wrong. I love writing for TV and I love being on set – working with actors, with a crew. Maybe because it's the most like theater. We're all in a room making something together. Except in TV, there is craft service. (laughs)

Same applies to screenwriters as well, doesn't it? There are very few who get continuous work in the movies.

Maybe. I don't know that much about the screenwriting world. Although, I think there are fewer people making a living as screenwriters period. I think it's a smaller pool of writers. For every movie, there's one maybe two or three writers. For every TV show there are six to 12. I like TV because I like working with other writers and it's a steady paycheck. And there are reruns. (laughs) For which you get checks in the mail that are like free money. They're like from Santa. Whenever we see those envelopes from the Writer's Guild, my husband and I are like kids on Christmas morning! "What'd we get?!" (laughs) There are a lot of reasons why I think TV is a better place for playwrights. Because if you've been in the theater where you are the most important person in the room and no one would be in that room unless the playwright put pen to paper in the first place...And you come from that and you go to the cinema, where you are not even invited to the set...it's a huge change in role. In TV even a staff writer goes on set. Has a say in the casting process. Meets one-on-one with the director and goes over the script with a fine-tooth comb.

So what you are saying is TV is like the theater, because it's a writer's medium.

Yes, absolutely. They're both dialogue-driven. Film is image-driven. What's that old saying? "A movie is a story told in pictures."

You think that's the reason? I mean, there's a lot on American TV right now which looks very cinematic. I mean, look at Boardwalk Empire *or* Breaking Bad.

Yeah, they are beautifully shot. They're shot to look as good as a movie. But the storytelling is still character-driven. The kinds of movies studios are making now are event movies or tentpole movies. Superheroes. Zombies. The world is ending. The world *has* ended. The White House is going to be hit by an asteroid. In 3D. They're big visual spectacles with lots of action that are expected to make so much money they can support the studio. I'm not a visual person … so I could never write one of those movies.

How was it to start at West Wing? *And how could such a show have even been produced?*

Even at that time Aaron Sorkin was a pretty established writer and John Wells was and is a huge producer, so I think the combination of those two guys is what sold it. John Wells is known to be an amazing manager, you know, he will say, "Your outline is due on Monday, your first draft is due two weeks after that, your second draft is due a week after that" … and those deadlines are met, let me tell you. (laughs). John is the owner of the factory and he keeps everything running on time. So, studios and networks trust him. He's going to keep the show running. But he also has great humanity. He's also a family man. He knows at the end of the day everyone wants to go home and see their kids. Aaron has a completely different style. If he's got a deadline coming up and he feels that he needs to go to Vegas overnight to clear his head, he'll do it.

So two opposites. Chaos and order.

Yes. I only worked on the first season so I don't know if they ever came up with a different way of working.

It looks like American TV is being written mainly by men and mainly white men.

Oh yes.

Why is that, you think?

I can only guess. But you have to consider first who says "I want to be a writer." You know it's a long shot. You know that the chances of you being successful are slim. And that you're going to spend years toiling away with no reward until someone "discovers" you. So, not a lot of people can afford to do that. Some writers have parents who can provide a safety net if things don't work out. But a lot of us don't. People like me, you know, who have immigrants for parents. Or whatever, just don't come from money. I never had any financial support from my parents once I graduated from college. I was teaching, I was waitressing, I had three jobs at a time. And I knew that if I was going to make it as a writer,

I was going to have to do it myself. No one could pick up the phone and make a call for me. Introduce me to a producer or a studio exec or someone who could open a door for me. I just had to sit in my East Village apartment and write. I had to write something good enough for people to notice me. Then the other thing you have to consider is who is making those hiring decisions. What are they responding to when they read a writer's work? Most execs and showrunners are white men and you know, we all respond to work that feels familiar to us. Comfortable. Whether we know it or not. There's a shared aesthetic, a shared interest or sense of humor. So, as long as white men are making the decisions then the majority of people they hire are going to be people who feel familiar to them. I feel incredibly lucky to have the career I've had and yes, if someone wanted to point to me and say "How can you say that? You get hired all the time and you're not a white man," they would be right! (laughs) There are definitely exceptions. So if I wanted to fluff myself up I could say that being a good writer is all that counts and I'm a good writer. And maybe that's true. I've gone from being a young woman writing experimental plays in my East Village walkup to being the primary breadwinner of my family.

That's great in so many ways.

Sure. Believe me, I count my blessings every day. But for some reason, it bothers me when people go "Oh, you're so lucky, you're doing so well, everything's great." It *is* great. I get paid to write and my kids get to see my name on the TV...let's face it, I'm not a coal miner. I have a fun job! (laughs) But I don't know, I just bristle when people make it seem like it's perfect. Nothing's perfect. I'd like to have more time to write plays, not every show is super fun to work on...sometimes I have to work in a different city than the one my family lives in...and I have to leave my husband behind with three boys. It's great...but it's not perfect.

Were you in a writers' room there?

Yes. Both shows that I had to commute for, *Southland* and *Do No Harm*, had writers' rooms. That's why I had to physically be there. It's doable but grueling. But worth it to keep my family in New York. I can't help it, I love New York! (laughs) You can be anonymous in New York. No one really cares that you write for a TV show here. You're just some jerk (laughs). Los Angeles is a one-industry town. I couldn't have this conversation with you if we were in L.A. I'd be worried about who was sitting at the next table – are they a writer? Are they a studio exec? Would they overhear something that would bite me in the ass?

The amazing thing is that you have films and series set in New York and they are written by people in Los Angeles.

You can tell.

You think so?

I can tell. But most of the country doesn't live in New York so they can't tell.

I know that there was no writers' room on Law & Order: Criminal Intent. *What about* The West Wing? *Was there a room there?*

No, because Aaron wanted to write all the scripts.

So you would write the first draft and he would take it and rewrite it?

We would write scenes.

Now that I've never heard of. How did that work?

How did it work? (laughs) You would be in your office doing research for like weeks, not sure what was going on. And then you'd get a knock on your office door. "Aaron wants everybody in the conference room in ten minutes." And you'd go and he'd say, "Hey guys, I'm late on the script and I've got nothing. What have you got?" And you'd say, "Well, I wasn't really given an assignment but I've done some research on school vouchers." And he'd say "Alright, what about school vouchers? What is it about them that is fascinating? What are the arguments?" And you'd go, "Well, the right thinks this, but the left thinks that and the interesting thing is..." And he'd say "OK, good, good, good. Write that." But we wouldn't know what that meant. "Am I writing the script? Am I writing the storyline? What am I doing?" So John Wells would say, "Go ahead and beat out that story. Figure out how it gets introduced in Act One, how it develops in Act Two, etc." But you wouldn't know what script it would go into. So you'd beat it out. It felt being like an overpaid researcher. Because you weren't writing. You were doing research and plotting. So then we decided what we would do is write the scenes. In isolation, which was hard... the storylines on that show were so interwoven and here you were writing them in isolation. And then we'd give them to Aaron and he would lay them out on the floor and bend over them and figure out how he would make them work, how he would weave them into a script.

This is a pretty amazing way to work. That is very much a single voice then. And still, I understand that Aaron was asked to leave The West Wing *after four seasons? Was that the reason?*

At some point Kevin Falls came on as an executive producer and I think some order was established. Aaron has quite openly said in the press that in the four years he was on the show, not a single episode was delivered on time or on budget.

What about Southland? *The process is entirely different when you have a proper writers' room, right? Do you like it more, or do you like it less?*

I'm not crazy about writers' rooms because…it's just too many brains, too many ideas. Too many voices at the table. But the way we did it on *Southland* was pretty good. We did not meet eight hours a day, which is how some shows do it. I've heard that on *Grey's Anatomy* they have, like, a treadmill and elliptical machine in the writers' room! Because they are there all day. But on *Southland* we would meet three days a week, for about three to four hours a day. Now, what's useful about that is that you would get your outline notes and your first draft notes at the table. So I could learn from someone else's outlines, what the producers liked and what they didn't like. But we didn't sit around and break story that much. We threw some ideas around but then the writer would go home to finish the outline themselves. So that was a pretty good use of the writers' room.

Sounds like you've had pretty mixed experiences.

But you know, overall I've been really lucky. I've had scripts produced that were untouched by the showrunner. And that's a good feeling. That feels like an accomplishment. Maybe it comes back to that whole "Oh, you write for TV? That's so great! You have it so great!" thing that just makes me feel like "Yes, it's great. Can we please stop talking about it now?" (laughs)

I guess you have to write in the voice of the show if you want your script to remain untouched? Can you explain what that means for a writer?

Every show has a voice. It's the voice of the showrunner. It's the style that the writer writes in. And as a writer on that show, it's your job to write in that style. You know, it's like if you're writing for *Law and Order*, you don't want to write in the style of *Mad Men*. Although there were times on *Law & Order: Criminal Intent* when I would write a line and I would think, "René[1] is going to love this. It sounds like a line he would write." And then, I'm in another scene, and I'd think, "Oh my

God, I am so tempted to write this line but I know that René will hate it, but to amuse myself I'm just gonna put it in." (laughs) And then, after René did his pass, I would find out that he rewrote the line I thought sounded just like him and he kept the line that was so me that I thought he wasn't going to like it. So, basically, you can never be right. (laughs)

If you could change one thing about the way American TV is being produced, what would that be?

You know, sometimes you get notes from the studio which are about the dramaturgy. They will say, this is open-ended here, can you close it up, or you didn't connect these two points in the storytelling that you could have. And those are great notes, those are great to get. But you also get notes like, "So, even though the victim's body is on the ground and the cop character says 'He has no pulse,' and we have seen the victim being hit by a car really badly, the cop never says, 'He's *dead.*' Can you change the line so the cop says, 'He's dead?'" And you go, "Well, he already said, 'He's got no pulse' and the victim's lying on the street, bleeding from his ears. So does he really also have to say, 'He's dead?' If you don't have a pulse, you're dead." (laughs) So, I feel like sometimes they want you to do things, "Can you make it clearer?" and you go, "It *is* clear."

So they want to make sure that every single member of the audience will understand, and that may be at the cost of subtlety?

That's right. And I think the audience is more intelligent than we give them credit for being.

More room for subtlety, more room for narrative experiments? Less notes?

(laughs) Narrative experiments ... that would be fantastic! In cable there are narrative experiments. I mean, *Southland* is very innovative. There are episodes where you don't even see the villain. It's groundbreaking really, for a cop show. And cable networks let writers create much more complicated characters than you can have on broadcast, where you need 12 million people to watch your show to keep it alive. Shows like *Homeland, The Americans, Breaking Bad, Boardwalk Empire* ... have really dark, complex, nuanced characters that don't have to be loveable and cuddly all the time. And those are the shows that I personally like to watch.

Charlie Rubin

Charlie Rubin has been a staff writer or writer-producer at *Seinfeld*, *The Jon Stewart Show*, *In Living Color* and *Law & Order: Criminal Intent*, among others. He created and runs the TV Writing Area at the Dramatic Writing Department of the Tisch School of the Arts. He is currently writing the movie *Brooklyn Surfers* for Robert Chartoff Productions (six *Rocky* movies, *The Right Stuff, Enders Game*).

Charlie, is it safe to say that you are the only tenured TV writing professor at university level in New York?

What matters is how I got here – that this school, Dramatic Writing, was willing, early on, to develop a specific curriculum focusing on TV writing as the equal of its writing programs in play and film. No other school was doing that. This school, however, had a built-in prejudice. It had one when I first came and it still has it to some extent. That theater was the important art and that screen was inferior but it was also slightly important. Television was nothing, television was garbage.

You started teaching TV writing in the fall of 1999, is that right?

Yes. And my feeling at the time was that TV writing had become superior to film writing and equal to prominent stage writing, of which there was very little, especially compared to all the outstanding TV series going on at the same time. I used to rattle those TV series off when we'd do "Meet The Freshmen" or something. One of the play teachers got angry with me and said, "Why do you do that, why do you always recite a list?" And I'd say, "Because I want TV students to take pride in hearing those names all together. You say Shakespeare, Shaw, O'Neill, Chekhov, and kids know what being a playwright means" and she said "But do *you* know what that means?" and I'd had it with this half-witted condescension, I just pointed at her and said, "RADIO. She's radio. Meet radio" and the room exploded and we both realized, they love TV. But of course, I was just being provocative. Because that's how you get people to listen to you, by going too far. And to some extent I was being nasty, implying that TV was where jobs were and you'd starve to death in theater. So I stopped doing that, I didn't like the person who did this – well, I liked him sometimes. We all like the idiot inside us. I liked him when they didn't invite me to a gala honoring our school's major donors because I might say something "pro-TV." Because now I knew we had them on the run.

Today, TV is the largest concentration at Dramatic Writing because students watch TV and see how good it is, season after season, and come in demanding more classes in it. But as recently as four or five years ago I was referred to around here as "one of these TV writers." TV was like the drooly cousin you fed in the kitchen while the serious relatives got served crack in the dining room. We've built this terrific concentration here, with about seven or eight or nine adjuncts, all working TV writers, teaching it, and yes, I'm the only full-time TV person. And when I started I would stand up and say, you all know how good television is, come in here and write it: "TV is more of an art form than the theater is now." Bit of an overstatement but theater was the bully you had to punch out on the playground to earn your place. Academia teaches this unholy godding up of the theater and The Play. And what I really wanted people thinking was: TV? Art form? Why not? Students now come out of here having learned how to write for television, and to respect it. Still, it used to be that they could find jobs more easily than they do now, now it's as hard to find a job in TV as anywhere else. And our playwrights, God bless them, they all take TV classes now, and they all plan TV series. Usually their first pilot is about a plucky group of actors or a plucky summer stock company of college students, but they get past that and their next pilot is battling robots. But the one *after* that will be damn good. Going back to the 1930s, poets could earn a high three-figure income while paying their bills teaching, which was wonderful, there was that place for them in academia, but somewhere along the road playwrights started saying, "Let's go into TV. We don't want to live like the poets of our generation, teaching." There's nothing wrong with teaching; I teach. I love it. But there are hardly any playwrights who can sustain themselves just from their playwriting. But hopefully by giving people here at Dramatic Writing a firm grounding in three kinds of writing, TV, stage, screen they'll find more opportunities to develop themselves as artists in some kind of professional context.

Playwrights do seem to have a new interest in TV right now.

These days young playwrights all want to work there. Instead of taking the traditional playwright step of doing your laundry in the gas station sink while struggling to get your plays up. No one's embarrassed by the medium anymore. When I started here, what I said was: if you want to go into TV, write a couple of spec scripts of current shows. That's what people wanted to read ten years ago. No animated shows, because Hollywood marginalized them. Then animation hit, so animation specs and pilots became OK. And then there was a revived interest in playwrights because the little agents were bored with specs. I couldn't blame them but too often the business is driven by the agents' boredom threshold. So there was an initial feeding frenzy. Then Hollywood was sold on the idea that pilots are good portfolio fodder. Let someone write a pilot and then we'll get a combination of how they might think as a playwright and yet see if they understand how television is structured. Here is what I tell my students: write a spec script, have a pilot and then have a third thing. It can be another pilot, it can be a play. The playwrights love to say that everyone in TV wants them. This is very untrue. People put these ideas out there, especially in a writing school where careerist ignorance can spread like the plague. "I heard a girl got onto *The Sopranos* by just submitting an idea for a short story." It's the old: I tell you something stupid, you tell it to someone else, it comes back to me and I say, "Hell. I heard that too!" There is also a tendency for some teachers to tell students information that resonates with their own fears of not having a legacy or to plump up their enrollments. One thing about the TV Concentration at DW, we don't need to advertise anymore. We don't promote. We don't have to. The cultural clock ticks and we move on. Art is wide enough for all of us to swim in it. But sooner or later, we are all radio.

In the long run, when this school functions, when it works well, I think we teach people how to write everything and you begin to discover what you're really good at. You know, academia keeps notions of the world going that are outdated by two generations. Academia is always two generations behind the history of thought and accomplishment. I like to hire people for the TV concentration who know things I don't know. I think when we teach TV here, we have to teach it as something that is global. I find that my best students here know what the Brits are doing, what's going on all over Europe or Latin America, they can watch everything online now. Thirty years ago the only sense we could have of TV outside of American network TV was Masterpiece Theater and every so often HBO would offer a show with a title like *Those Crazy Japanese Guys*. And we would see some of these things they would do, sitting in tubs full of ice water. Game shows where you bury your girlfriend and try to find her a year later. They had that wonderful so far out there, yet repressed sexual longing, that the Japanese society is full of. I think the TV industry is much more inclusive today, and much more willing to take chances than the other arts are. It doesn't mean that almost everything you see on TV isn't a variant of a certain kind of formula but the potential of the high end of that formula is with us now in ways that it never was before. If F. Scott Fitzgerald was trying to drink himself to death in Hollywood today he'd be doing it on the staff of *Justified*.

You've written for the movies, been a playwright-in-residence, done TV comedy and drama. What's harder?

I always think that *whatever I'm doing* is the hardest medium to be in. I did four years of *Law and Order: Criminal Intent* and when I was ready to leave for a movie, I had to unlearn everything I learned at *Criminal Intent* that I spent years getting good at and occasionally mediocre at, how you move scenes and distribute information, the briskness of scenes, how the Act One act break is always, "We got nothing." One-hour police procedurals, how every scene is shaped by the simple idea of, "What do the cops want to learn? What do they know, or think they know?"

One could argue that one can do more in theater.

I think that's one of those notions that theater perpetuates about itself, whatever "do more" means. What are we comparing here, Shakespeare to an art form that didn't show up until 1946? The Greeks had a template they wrote into just the way a police procedural does. There have been innovative works of art in TV in every era, there are just more of them today. Theater people love to define themselves by their best, over 2000 years. But TV they define by its worst. There's a brilliant old book about TV called *Seven Glorious Days, Seven Fun-Filled Nights* where a guy named Charles Sopkin watches TV for pretty much every minute of a week in April, 1967, and takes encyclopedic notes. It's meant to confirm the "vast wasteland" take on TV but I dare anybody to read this thing and not feel that art is flashing by with all the sewage.

In TV you get a lot of cop stuff, you get a lot of goofy-goofy, you get a lot of doctors but in the long run it's an experimental medium. I also think that in ten years or so there's going to be a blooming in theater. We're going to have a high theater art period like we haven't had since the 1960s and the reason is going to be that playwrights are being educated in TV writing. They used to go into TV after they felt that they couldn't get a production anymore, so the poor defrocked playwright would lower himself and go to California to be gloriously bitter on *Lost in Space*. What is happening now is that people who come to schools like this to study playwriting very quickly discover that they can learn how to write for TV too and that they are likelier to get work for their first years as TV writers, and then maybe they're gonna make some money and then they'll leave. And of course some will stay forever, O let us weep for the playwright who's traded up for an audience of millions! But I'm talking about those people who are committed to the stage, they just feel it so deeply – and what will happen is they're gonna go out and write TV and put money in the bank but one day they're gonna leave and they'll spend the next ten years writing plays. And they will write great plays. They will write plays better for all the time that they spent in TV. They'll come back and they'll have learned all those kind of lessons and they'll be able to afford to work for the theater. That's my prediction, somewhere around 2020 we're going to see an amazing flowering in the theater. I just feel it. It used to be fail in theater, fail in movies, go to TV. Now it'll be succeed in TV, succeed in theater.

What a great thought! And what about original production for the internet? There's a lot happening right now, especially in New York.

I think the internet has given us the current explosion in sketch and improv. Net stuff works better in short gulps, and with so many sketch kids and comedy types having, essentially, an editing studio in their Macs, the quality of the finished sketches is exceptional. I'd rather watch *College Humor* or *Funny Or Die* than *Two Broke Girls*, or most "webisodes" that are essentially people auditioning to staff up on *Two Broke Girls*. Today submitting a webisode is like a half-hour writing sample, though, beware, the conservative industry often goes to its "Yeah but did *one* person write this, or was it a gang-bang?" place. Another huge change coming in TV is that as our home TVs keep getting bigger, TV will finally start using backgrounds. It's not gonna just be, "Tell the extras director to get people moving on the damn bank line in the background!" anymore, they're gonna actually use the backgrounds to help us tell the story. We're already getting to that place in some cable shows. What I see on the web, it's funny but it's small, you can't attract the talent; that makes it cheaper, of course. I sense the enthusiasm for the web stuff comes from the financial model it could perhaps represent one day. Why have a cast of ten in a show like *House* if people will watch a cast of three and accept six minutes of it? *Girls* is essentially a web show that blew up and skipped the web. Because it has such a wide personal focus I think it's an exciting modeling for the future of TV. Though it's depressing. I thought *my* twenties were depressing. Now I see they were all puppy dogs all the time.

What did you like most while working on Criminal Intent?

I worked for two different EP's (Executive Producers), René Balcer, who created the show, and then Warren Leight. And with both of them there was always the sense that every week they wanted to top last week's show. Being a writer on a high-end show like *Criminal Intent* is exhaust-ing. You know, a show where there's an arc for a season, where there are a lot of characters to move around. It's a procedural, so there are all the ways that procedurals work, where you move the information – "carry the water," as Vince D'Onofrio used to say. What writing for TV is about is accepting that you have to find yourself within someone else's vision. Which includes their limitations and the genre's or characters' limita-tions. People always miss that about a long-running show. They think it's easy, you plug the characters in from week to week. You go to par-ties and you meet accountants who'll say, "My job's harder than yours. Everyone's tax return is different." Anyhow I loved procedurals but once I left and *CI* brought in Jeff Goldblum I never watched it again, it felt like cheating on my wife. *The Simpsons* and *South Park* are the only shows I watch every week. They're brilliant, the best shows in the history of TV. Well, I love *Combat!* and *St. Elsewhere* too, but I think my heart is always in comedy. Dick Wolf used to complain to Warren, "Charlie still thinks he's in sitcoms." Rene once told a room of actors, "Here's the only guy who's written for *Seinfeld* and *Criminal Intent.*" And the actors gave me this look like, "Wow. We'll respect you for ten seconds for that." It was closer to eight.

Isn't it The Simpsons *where they had two writers' rooms writing the same episode at the same time?*

Not that I know of. I thought that there was a story pitch and someone wrote a draft and they brought it to the table where all the other writers are. The only show I know of that did what you say was *Roseanne*. She had three writers' rooms, not two. And they would often write the same episode and they'd each have their own person running the table. It was said that she tended to hire pleasant, well-adjusted table-runners so that she would have someone to abuse. By the way, it's an absolutely great show, even if she was one of these mean people I'm glad I missed work-ing for. I had Carol Burnett for that slot. America's favorite mop lady was OK but she hired incompetent producer-monsters which, I would submit, made her a monster herself.

So how did you learn writing?

I had three great writing teachers at Horace Mann School and only two of them later ended up on a list of the school's accused pedophiles. After college I went into publishing, I edited books. But I'd always had an idea for a musical that Bill Finn, who later wrote *Falsettoland*, wanted me to write. And it was a pretty interesting time, and we did this show and we couldn't pull it together, the music was wonderful, but some nights people sat on their hands. I was a wreck, it felt like a disaster of amazing proportions. I don't think it really was, still…There's nothing like an audience not laughing. Or an audience not getting what you're doing, even if they are laughing. Then a couple of editors from the *National Lampoon* saw it, and they asked me to write for their humor magazine and I began doing that. So many people from that time are still my friends, it was 1983 or '84…That's where I really learned how to write. It was like a pre-op writers' room.

There were seven or eight of us who were the core team and in spite of the massive age discrimination in Hollywood we're all still working. We were that good, sorry to say that, but we were. Still, we couldn't get people to read the magazine. Later on I did journalism, I wrote sports for a while, I was the sports columnist of *The Village Voice*, I did all these things. And what happened was these seven or eight guys at the *National Lampoon* – we didn't all like each other, but we liked each other's work – we all began recommending each other for jobs. So I got the first TV job I was put up for, and that was a Cinemax talk show "hosted" by Max Headroom, a computer animation projection who'd interview celebrities. The producer of the show, Bob Morton, who also produced *Letterman* had decided to hire two American and two British writers. But you know, first job is easy to get; it's the second job that's the really tough one. Because your second job is based on your first job and for your first job you're somebody's find and they'll tell people you're a genius because it makes them look like a genius at finding. I got this first job on *Max* over all these guys with more experience, because I was new, they hadn't heard of me yet, and I was cheap. And I'm at the Xerox machine and I'm reading this stuff of the other American guy and I'm thinking, man, this guy is good, this guy is better than I am. That was Larry David. When people ask me how do you break into TV, I say the secret is, on your very first show, try to have your office next to the guy who's going to create *Seinfeld*. We hit it off. He taught me that the experienced guy should be good to the new guy, so he came in to talk to me, he was incredibly generous. And we went out to lunch every day, and we almost got fired together when Max introduced "our next guest, Mary Tyler Moore," with a stream-of-consciousness monologue about the shit-stains on his underpants. It was so pointlessly mean that everyone assumed we *had* to have written it. But it was an ad-lib, and Larry ultimately hired me onto *Seinfeld*. He also gave me a compliment one day – and since here I was, I'd been funny in various places but I was new to TV, I was pretty insecure. I was in a stand-up club with some sad birds from MTV and Larry spotted me. He was going on next. And he told me, well – that I had to leave. I thought he was kidding – no. I *had* to leave, I couldn't be in his audience. He wouldn't go on. Go! He said, "I cannot do my act in front of someone I respect." So I left. And it made me feel good because someone I respected threw me out of the club. Still does.

How was that experience, Seinfeld?

I think there are two shows in recent American TV history where the writers who worked on them never get over them. If you worked on *SNL* in its first few years, or on *Seinfeld*, it's always gonna be the part of your resume that jumps out to people and they always want to know about it and about nothing else. Even *The Letterman Show* never reached that point; these two shows are totem shows. Even if I was only there for a season, it was incredibly formative. Larry Charles, another great writer on that show, taught me how to pitch, he saved my job, he saved my life. He told me once, "You're the first person I've met who hates his grandfather as much as I hate mine." So that was a comedy bond. L.C. taught me how to pitch to *Seinfeld*. He'd say things like, "If you can write that scene so Jerry gets to lose control, that's one of the things he likes to do as an actor, and nobody ever writes it." Ron Hauge, my great writing partner, had been doing all our pitching. He was fast and fearless but Larry C told me to take over because my personal style, losing my place, forgetting things, stepping on my punchline, was "more the *Seinfeld* style."

Did you have a writers' room?

No. You went to Larry and Jerry. You told them an idea. And 19 times out of 20 they told you no – automatically. Yeah, it's good, but what else have you got? What else have you got? And eventually there were two or three things that they would really almost like. And they'd say, "Ok, so that's your Kramer and that's George and Jerry, this Elaine is not a story, go to the index cards." This is the old, no, the end of the old days. You'd get some index cards and you'd go to the corkboard and you'd start pushpinning them up. You know, Act One, Act Two. You'd use different colors for each act and say, now I am truly a professional. And then Larry and Jerry would come in and they'd start moving the cards around. Today you break story on the white board, or electronically, at *Seinfeld* you did it with the cards. And then you went off and you wrote a couple of drafts, and at a certain point they'd say, "We're gonna take it away from you." And they would rewrite it. It tended to be that the more they liked it the quicker they took it. Though sometimes what they liked meant the idea, not what you were doing with it. Let's be honest.

That was a NYC show shot in L.A., right?

It was all done on the Studio City lot, but every so often they'd fly a guy in, in a Kramer wig, to run down the subway stairs and be shot from behind. I never stopped missing New York. Most New York writers in L.A. whine, "Ohh. I miss New York. But now I prefer a gated community."

But the writers were all based here?

No. Wrong. One of the things that made the *Law and Order* shows work was that they were all shot here, in New York. Our show, *Criminal Intent*, and *Law and Order*, the mothership, were based at Chelsea Piers. We were New York people who wrote New York types. I think it's unfortunate that there aren't more shows in New York, and the reason why the networks don't want to do that is that they would have to fly out here to make a trip to the set. Executives want to be able to say, "Well, I'm gonna go take my lunch over at the studio, and watch my show." And then they hang around for five hours, talking about how they ran over a guy once and kept going, getting in people's way, and then they go home. Meanwhile everyone else stays up, does the show. Yes, I'm a little prejudiced, but people want to control things. And the studios in Los Angeles don't like shows in New York, because they can't control them. Anyway, I left *Criminal Intent* for a screen deal, and the first draft I wrote sounded like the best *Criminal Intent* I ever wrote. It was who I'd become. There's a guy who's been one of *Letterman's* monologue writers for many years, he found what he wants to be and he's great at it, so he stays. But it doesn't work for me. My motto has always been, if you can't get fired, quit.

There is a notion that the secret of success of American TV lies with the writers' rooms.

I think that people who think that that's where the quality of American TV comes from, are nuts. In fact there are good writers' rooms and good room-shows but there's *never* only one way to do a show. If *The Simpsons* is a room show, as they say, it's the best show in the history of TV. A friend of mine worked on *Cheers* at the very end. There were four writers who ran the show and there were another four guys who composed the staff. Every week the four guys who ran the show took one of the four new guys into the inner sanctum and taught them how to run the show as they broke and rewrote that week's episode. Four guys training four guys to replace them. Brilliant. In the year I was on *Seinfeld*, I think there were four writers' meetings, tops, I can almost remember what each was about. And one was about, "Look, anything marked JERRY in the refrigerator is Jerry's. Don't handle it. Jerry doesn't like his food handled." It usually was something like, "I thought midgets would be funnier, I can't believe we're not gonna get more laughs on midgets, let's beef up the Elaine story, any ideas?" And that was how they did the show, through the strong presence of Larry and Jerry. *Criminal Intent* didn't have a room under René, under Warren … sometimes he'd tour around asking everybody what did they think? Then he'd close himself in with his brain trust, Tommy Lasorda and Earl Weaver. *Two and a Half Men* I'm told is indeed Chuck Lorre and ten writers in the room. That's how he likes to run it. But not every show runs that way. My own prejudice as someone who is funny but can write serial killers too: I'm not a room guy, which is strange since I am teaching and have to be the center of the room while not being it. I have no idea what I mean by that. On *Seinfeld* I was probably one of the quietest guys ever. But I taught myself how to stand up in a room on shows, over time, and in that way, teaching has made me a better writer and a better producer. I'm a much better writer for *Seinfeld* now, years later, than I was when I was there. I should send some scripts in and see if they get bought. 50–50.

There's a writers' room depicted in 30 Rock. *Are the writers close to reality?*

It's like Hollywood's version of what a writer is. Writers tend to be dull. They can be funny with each other but that's it. I love that show, but *The Office* changed television and could break your heart too.

What do you ask your students to write at Dramatic Writing?

For a one-hour spec, I like to have them write things that I like and can stand to watch. I can break anything down but I have to like it. I like them doing *Breaking Bad, Friday Night Lights* when it was on, *Mad Men* – and this was really astonishing to me, they're so good at writing that. Somehow students who are so far from the 60s, they do the research, you know, how the Volkswagen came to this country, what Nabisco crackers people were eating, they enjoy finding out stuff about that time. But when they try to write *Entourage*, they don't know anything about Hollywood and producers and agents. Just what they see in movies and TV. *30 Rock* they're weak at. Same reason as *Entourage*. What do they know about putting up a daily show? *The Office* is easier for them to write because most of them have had some low-level experience in dull businesses during the summer. *Girls* is a hot spec now. It takes the creepiness vibe of *Sex and the City* and goes platinum with it, so young writers love it. Young writers should always go creepy. Go too far. And go creepy.

With specs, do you tell them to write into the season being broadcast at the moment?

The reverse. I tell them to pick a point in the past of the show. Let's say *Mad Men*. If you write into a spot two or three seasons ago, it should help you to know that at a certain point the firm is going to move and at a certain point a division will take place, so half of them will go one way and half of them will go another. If you write into the current season you're basically playing "match wits with the writing staff." If you have a great idea, chances are someone on the staff is having it too and you'll see it on the screen one night and then desperately apply to law school so you can go into business affairs at the studios and start screwing other writers. Anyway, *Mad Men* is perfect, because it had an 18-month gap between Season One and Season Two. Put your episode there.

The pilot script and spec script are basically calling cards, right?

Right, but you have to stress that nobody is going to buy their spec script for the ongoing series. And tell kids writing pilots that you don't need to include a breakdown of the whole season. That's outsmarting yourself, crazy thinking, that's 1971 thinking; your single, 32–33-page pilot is all you need. Nobody is going to buy your pilot, but they may buy you off it, and five years from now or eight years from now, when you're successful and more powerful, maybe you'll get this pilot done, but right now ... it's magic thinking to think you'll hit it overnight. Sometimes there's too much magic thinking at a writing school. With pilots, what I say to them is, tell me what it's about, now tell me who the star is – the role that gets it bankrolled – now tell me who the most important secondary character is, the antagonist, tell me who the third most important character is, now these three are going to bring all the stories, and that's all we work on. Tell me what is the dead hot center of the show. When you get to the end of this pilot, the reader should say, "Well, I can imagine loads more stories." Also think about what's the show really about? Like *Frasier* is really about the brothers proving their masculinity to themselves and each other and their cop dad. The core of the show *Weeds* is Nancy thinking, "I'm the best mother in the world, because I became a drug dealer to support my family." And the best moments of that show are where she realizes "Damn, I'm the worst mother in the world. Look what I've done, look what I've exposed my kids to." Writers being what they are, they will sometimes go off and write spec scripts about a useless secondary character. They think that's a cool pro angle. But the thing is, the secretary is the secretary, don't go write stories about her, who cares? Or you have this elaborate fantasy about getting hired onto the show because you had the brains to give the secretary more than one line, so she falls for you! And as a teacher, I try to give them this important advice, "She will still sleep with a bartender. Not you." Focus on the star and one other important character – Michael and Dwight, Hannah-Adam. People used to show up at agents' offices and say, "I created a series and I have the first 20 episodes right here!" Craziness. No one wants to read all that shit from a newbie. They want to read one episode and see if they can imagine themselves into the others that will follow. Writers are always so self-destructive. Because we create. And think creation and self-destruction are the same thing. Anyway, it's worked for me. Writers will revere the teacher-mentor who tells them to write 40 episodes to sell a series, but who leaves out, "This is why I am teaching eighth grade biology."

What about the Catch-22 of Hollywood? What about agents and managers?

I don't believe in managers until you're successful. Students love them because they will take you on quicker than an agent will. As the Dramatic Writing TV wing has gotten well-known, managers have offered me money just to flip them the scripts of the most talented kids here, something that I'm not gonna do. A manager will say, "What if I take all of your TV concentrates, all the seniors. I'll take 15 kids and throw them out there, and 14 of them will be ruined, but one of them will be good." Whereas agents are uncouth, they're vulgar, often snaky – except mine, who is very sweet. An agent will say to me, "If you tell me you'd hire this girl, I'll read her. But if I hate her I won't trust you next time." Because agents are in it for the long run. Agents look for talent and occasionally know it. Managers look for volume.

Do you put your students in contact with agents?

Every so often. Most graduates aren't ready to be staffed. Some people are very close. I encourage them all to give themselves a three-year plan. During that time work for Starbucks, drive the Mr. Softy truck, keep working on your specs, fix your pilot, join writers' groups, and at the end of the three years your career has either started or you need to re-evaluate. You should probably be evaluating earlier than that. Why are you not hitting the target you have set out for yourself? Is it your spec, is it you when you meet people? And if you feel everyone's wrong about you, give yourself another couple of years. Very few people become a writer when they want to be. And not everyone becomes a writer, even after they've been to writing school. I wish that they did. I like the students here enormously. I always tell them, have a day job, because it's good to be around real people. You have to be in the real world somehow, you have to have those experiences, it's all part of becoming a writer. I think TV writers are by far smarter than playwrights. Some playwrights are so self-involved. And they have to stop using the word "voice" and "signature". One kid told me her play teacher advised her to spend all summer working on her voice. I told her, "I'm spending all summer working on my jumpshot. Let's get together at halftime and see who did better."

There are fewer TV movies now. Why do you think that is?

They used to be great. Absorbing, insightful. *I Know My First Name Is Steven*. *The Marcus-Nelson Murders*, that became *Kojak*. I hope they'll be back. It is so expensive to make just two hours of TV right now. And everyone knows the money is in the series. Everyone wants 100 episodes. Only the big shows go into syndication now when it used to be that everything, all of *BJ and the Bear*, would get syndicated.

So what do you show in class? Clips from the whole series?

No, this school is too expensive to turn class into a clip show, why waste that time when the kids can be workshoping their scripts in the room. Maybe once a term I'll discuss a pilot they've all watched in advance. If a show doesn't work or does, you can mostly see the reasons right there in the pilot. In the last class sometimes I'll show *Wonderland* from 2000, the best pilot I've ever seen, way ahead of its time, dark, brutal, complex, funny. It's about Bellevue Hospital: mental health professionals and patients who are vividly destabilizing and taking their docs with them. They only made eight and only ran two. It got the kind of review in The New York Times you wait your whole career for. And then two weeks later it was yanked, replaced by *BJ and the Bear*.

Tim Van Patten

Tim Van Patten's television credits as a writer and/or director include *The Sopranos, The Wire, Deadwood, Boardwalk Empire, Rome, The Pacific, Game of Thrones, Ed* and *Sex and the City*. He has won, among others, two WGA and two DGA awards, an Edgar, a Hugo, a Peabody, two Emmys and an AFI award.

Tim, you have a very multifaceted career. And you have a longstanding creative partnership with Terence Winter.

Indeed! But we're like two ships passing, Terry and I, I mean at the moment. He's really focused on the room and I'm focused on production. And sometimes we collide in the middle.

Boardwalk Empire *looks like cinema. Is that how you look at it, as a long cinematic narrative?*

It's a 12-hour movie.

And you are directing it. You have written an episode but mostly you are directing.

(laughs) Some of it. I start shooting on the 21st of January. I've committed to two episodes back to back. It's the first episode of Season Two. Tom (Fontana) and I have the same mentor. We were raised in the business by Bruce Paltrow. And Matt (Weiner) and Terry and I were raised by David Chase in *Sopranos*.

And you and Terry wrote a much acclaimed episode for The Sopranos.

That was a story that was related to my life, and Terry magically turned it into a great episode.

Talk to me about the scope of Boardwalk. *It certainly belongs to the projects with the biggest production values ever in the TV series world.*

Rome was big. And *Deadwood*. And *The Pacific*. That was massive. In some ways more massive productionwise than this show. Not as detailed storytelling, though. This is more complicated storytelling. That was more massive in terms of physical production.

I think *Pacific* was bigger because we covered a lot of ground in Australia. We shot up North, we shot up South, we created the geography of five different islands, we had to do Melbourne in period, we had an enormous number of extras and special effects and visual effects, so in terms of physical production *Pacific* was probably bigger. In *Boardwalk*

Empire we are confined to the boroughs of New York City. So that plane is a little bit smaller. But every bit as detailed, if not more, because we are working within the five boroughs of NYC physically but we are portraying New York City, Atlantic City, Chicago and in the coming season Philadelphia in 1920–1921. The challenge is that there is very little physical reminiscence of 1920–1921, so you can't just walk into anywhere and shoot, it has to be dressed, and you need visual effects to erase something or add something. We built the boardwalk in Brooklyn on an empty lot, surrounded by blue screen. The challenges are enormous but we are working at the studio and so we're not out in the elements as much.

How many shooting days do you have per episode?

Twelve, plus one concurrent day. And of those 13 days, in the first season we had probably eight on the studio. Again, we were chasing a tax rebate in New York, so to get the best rebate you have to stay within the five boroughs. When you think about what you're accomplishing, it is short. Unlike a network hour where you have commercials, with a cable show you're delivering an extra 15–20 minutes of film. They're really long days and it is a big cast. At any given time there's 25 regular characters, it's a very complex show and it's incredibly detailed in the world of wardrobe and production design and props, and so it's driven by those things.

There must be a lot of research involved.

Yes. We have a researcher who is in Atlantic City, we have the author of the book at our disposal, we have a department of people whose job is to identify period buildings and all sorts of detail and when we started, I'm sure Terry told you this, when we started on the pilot with Mr. Scorsese… He was really involved in terms of the overall look and feel of the show, and so he had Terry and I and sometimes a department head if the film was being focused on for that department, and we would watch films with him as references.

And what did he show you?

Oh my gosh, he had a list. It was like a school. Terry and I would pinch each other, like, I don't believe it, we're watching a film with Martin Scorsese. Just us three in the theater. Sometimes he would talk throughout the film: "Watch this film, it's a wonderful picture." And he knows every single detail of it. We would watch all types of films, sometimes we would wonder why we go over to watch this movie. We'd go to his office in the city, you know it's above the DGA [Directors Guild of America] building, he lives in the city. And he has his own little theater there. He just knows every little thing about every film that got made, so it was like an education. We would go sit down there and it was like a little escape, usually a double feature. Afterwards it's like, Marty, why did we even watch this movie? And he would say, "You see the scene with the carnival, wonderful, wonderful scene." And it was a small scene, but he would say, "That's how the boardwalk should be, the night light," and you'd go, yeah, he's right. A whole movie for a little detail. Like he would bring in the wardrobe person and have him watch a whole movie just for some little detail. This is something Terry and I had experienced at *Sopranos* as well, with David Chase. He really paid attention to detail.

Did you watch movies with him too?

No. Doing this pilot with Martin Scorsese was above and beyond any experience Terry and I had ever had. The schedule was longer, the budget was bigger. We really wanted to make it work. We built eight models of it and we'd bring models to him. It was a great undertaking.

So did you work with him on the pilot?

Yes, I would be out scouting locations, we would narrow down, we would try to keep it really streamlined and productive.

Is he still involved?

Yeah. We send him the scripts and he will give us notes. I think he really likes the show. And his notes are always dead on. As we watched all sorts of films, we watched Sam Fuller's *Park Row*, *Roaring Twenties*, *Luciano*. I wish we could keep doing it, every week.

You started as an actor, right?

Yeah. I was a bad actor (laughs). No, seriously, I realized very quickly that my interest was not in front of the camera. As an analogy I guess you could say, in baseball the catcher is in every single play, as an actor I felt like I was in the outfield, occasionally a ball would get out there, I wasn't in every play. The catcher controls the game by telling the pitcher what to pitch. It's just that sort of, I love the camaraderie spirit of the shooting crew, it's my family, and I have a great appreciation for the actors.

When did you start?

I started acting in the 70s, as a teenager in a show called *The White Shadow*, it was produced by Bruce Paltrow. Gwyneth was a baby when we were shooting, and he was my mentor, and then started me as a director as well. He started Tom Fontana as a writer. I mean, Tom was a playwright. He'd seen a play of Tom's and he took him on, and they worked on *St. Elsewhere* together. And not just us. I tell you, if you could see how far Bruce's influence was in this business, it was vast. That's a subject unto itself. The talented and awarded writers that came out of his world – it's astounding. He could identify talent and he knew how to manage talent. He was a great storyteller and leader but his strength was producing, he knew how to handle the networks, he was incredibly committed and he believed in what he was doing. Real honest and tough, tough as nails. Special. Go whisper it, Bruce's generosity. Television is a very insular business, very difficult business to penetrate if you come from the outside. You had to just sort of start as an insider, you'd have to be an actor or a script supervisor or first AD [assistant director]. Bruce was brilliant at it. Tom has done the same thing. He started an amazing amount of people. He is the most generous person I've ever met. And I'm trying to do it here. Keep moving people up. It's a great legacy. I believe in sharing information. What's the point otherwise? I think it's wrong if people covet information. It's an incredibly creative place to be, in a room full of writers.

So how do you work in relation to the script?

On this show it's a little different for me because I'm also an executive producer, and I'm so lucky because I'm on a show with my best friend. On *The Wire* I was an itinerary director who showed up to shoot a show, so you're not as close to the show. If you're just a director for hire, you show up. They put a script in your hands, you hit the ground running because it's an hour show so it's between seven and ten days, and you have seven to ten days of prep. You meet your first AD, you scout very quickly.

There comes a time in that prep period where you will have what they call a tone meeting, the director will sit down with the writer of the show and run through the script. On *Sopranos* that was very detailed. Some shows are not that detailed, it's just if you have any questions you can ask them. And some shows you have to walk through every scene, talk about the tone of the scene, you know, the nature of the scene, what the actors want, what is happening, how it relates to the rest of the series. It can be as detailed or as vague. This is very early on in the prep, and the very last thing is the reading. And you have to nail down locations and figure out the schedule. You will then have a read-through. And not all the shows have this either. I only started to experience this when

I came to work for HBO. And then after that read-through on the last day or the second last day, there will be a notes session for the writers. And the tone meeting... You sit down with the writer-producer and the writer of the episode, the line producer, first AD and run through the script and trade notes or suggestions and that will be the time to give them. On *Sopranos* that tone meeting would happen in the middle of your prep and the director called it "defending your life," because you would go in there and normally the writer would go through the script and you would sort of take notes and it was a lot of pressure. It was very stressful, because you had to say how you were going to approach the scene, what you thought it meant.

So what would happen, if you said something wrong?

It's much easier the other way around, when the writer works you through the script. And working on *Boardwalk Empire*, we followed the *Sopranos* method of tone meetings. And it works. It works really well. I'm here all the time; if I'm not directing, if I'm not on set, I'm casting or in the room.

Are you in the writers' room as well?

Yes, I am. Terry would be leading the room, I would come in and out. And we would talk about the season and which characters, talk about themes, it's up on the board, and then we'd start talking about each episode, beat to beat. And after that would come an outline, scene by scene, and that outline is assigned to a writer and the writer goes and writes. The process before anyone gets assigned a script could be three months. So, first episode has just come in, a writer goes away with an outline and comes back with a draft in three weeks. Maybe Terry gets it first.

So what if it doesn't work?

It would be addressed and the writer gets another one or two passes and if that doesn't work, then Terry gets a pass.

What would you say is your best and biggest tool?

My life. (a beat) Terry and I, we lived in very similar ways in Brooklyn, in fact our families are buried 100 yards from each other. Very strange. Very often we have the same sense of humor, we both reply almost like twins, we say exactly the same jokes.

Margaret Nagle

Margaret Nagle was a writer and supervising producer on HBO's *Boardwalk Empire*. Prior to that she created her own show *Side Order of Life* and wrote HBO's awarded television movie *Warm Springs* and the feature film *The Good Lie* for Warner Brothers. She has won two WGA awards.

So in terms of TV writing, everything is pretty much in Los Angeles?

It pretty much is. Except for Tom Fontana (laughs). He is a very special man. And I've never met him. But he is sort of the heart and soul of New York TV and all of the writers who have gotten to work under him have been so lucky and had incredible training. It's not sink or swim. He takes new writers and teaches them the craft. So he is a very mentoring and a very kind guy and his arm is really long-reaching in terms of all the writers. Like people will pitch me a writer and they'll say it's a Tom Fontana writer, he worked with Tom and I'll go, Oh OK. There's a stamp that he puts on his writers that is really great.

You know the staffs are in L.A. for the most part, because the buyers are in L.A. The networks and the studios are in L.A. But the tax credit that was enacted a couple of years ago in New York state has made shooting here much easier. That's why there's so many shows here. If they take the tax credit away, there will be nothing in New York. On *Law and Order* they have their own way of doing it, they split the writers' rooms, but mostly the writers rooms are in L.A. It's better to be closer to the set for changes and so on. If you have your scripts out in advance you can be further away, I think, but if you are writing on the fly ... You know, this writers' room also began in L.A.

It did?

They always said it would move to New York though. And I had another project that was "greenlit" before *Boardwalk*. So I left *Boardwalk* before it came to New York. And then it came to New York and they shot the first season and I wasn't here, and I didn't come at the beginning of this season. So I'm here sort of, I don't know, to consult, whatever my title is, I think it's supervising producer.

So what does that mean? Supervising producer?

The titles mean different things on different shows. I have a show I was executive producer on. We were talking about Tom Fontana. He has a way of delegating authority in this world, like for example Ed Zwick and Marshall Herskovitz who created *Thirtysomething* as well as a show from the mid-70s called *Family*. They pretty much produce everything and the writers write. But the writers do not break the story in a writers' room, they break the story with Marshall and Ed and they go off and write. Which is a little bit of the *Law and Order* model. On a network show the schedule is so much quicker. Time is everything in television. It's a ticking clock all the time, and you have a deadline and there is an air date. The train leaves the station, it doesn't wait for you. You need your writers to produce badly. You can't possibly, if you're at the top of it, do it all. Some personalities can delegate and some can't. Which means that the same title means different things, depending on the show. Supervising producer on this show also means I'll go to some casting sessions. Or I'll discuss the shooting schedule. We just had something where we needed to flip around the shooting schedule to accommodate one actor. So I said, we'll take the first week and we'll shoot all scenes with this one actor for the first four episodes we have written. Then he is free for four months. And on top of that let's pull all the scenes from the first four episodes we have written and let's pair them down a little bit so we know we can have them all shot. There's a production problem and you look at how you can solve it with the writing. So if I'm in the writers' room and someone says, all right, we're gonna blow up a boat, then you go, we don't have enough money in our budget to blow up the boat.

Where do you obtain the knowledge necessary to become a producer?

You learn it by doing. I executive produced 13 episodes of my own show, *Side Order of Life*, and I had a fabulous line producer, a guy named Charlie Goldstein who had been president of production for a TV studio. He had a broad-based resume and is one of the best line producers in the business, which is the person responsible not only for creating a budget, but making sure that it's adhered to once a show is up and running. Someone like Charlie knows exactly what everything is going to cost. They know how long it's gonna take. You can literally go into their office and they'll know it all off the top of their heads. For a TV writer, a great line producer is your best friend. You have a budget like you have with your life. It's exactly the same with the show. It's fun.

Where does the writing come in?

I am a supervising producer on the whole show. Terry is the showrunner, which is the person totally in charge just as David Chase was on *The Sopranos*. It's all about his taste, point of view, his voice, his eye, he's the architect of this great, big beautiful house with many rooms. And I may decorate the kitchen but it's Terry Winter's vision. We try and help him. The best writer-producer is always one that is writing the same show that the creator has in their head. What makes a successful staff is that everybody is writing the same show. You're all building the same house. So Terry may say design a kitchen but I have to design a kitchen that goes with his worldview. So he's got this point of view about the 1920s and these characters and who they are and they are all born out of his vision, he is inside these characters. So my job is to try to understand where he's going. And then if I have a new idea or I say let's take the Manhattan Bridge instead of the Brooklyn Bridge, I need to be able to stand up and say why that fits into where we're going or why I think we are ready to take a different bridge at this moment in the storytelling. So you have to be able to propose things and you have to be able to defend things and oftentimes no one wants to hear it. We take these vast notes, do we need that scene, I take notes too, there is someone who takes notes, but I take notes too. I hear different things. And what happens is these notes become an outline.

Who writes the outline?

Terry.

He writes the outline?

He likes to write the outline. It's like running it through his own computer, and then we sit and go through the outline.

This is a scene by scene breakdown, right?

We do the stories of each character. And then you want to figure out how do these characters fit together. So we may lift out a storyline belonging to Margaret, which does not work in a certain episode and we keep it for another episode, because it's a story we really want to tell about her. The show is evolving, but it's not time yet to tell that story.

So you meet every day?

From ten to six, yes.

And then you have an outline. And each one of you gets assigned an episode? And when do you do the writing?

Terry sends you off. He gives you some time out of the writers' room. He usually gives a week or two weeks. You do that at home or in the office, you shut the door. On my show I would make the writers write their outlines themselves and then I would work with them but I really like outlines. Terry has so many masters he has to serve. He has to serve HBO with all these outlines. HBO is not gonna give me notes on the outlines, they're gonna give them to Terry. So he has a hard job, because he has to facilitate us, facilitate them, facilitate the cast and crew, and the production; it's a really hard job.

The time when you're out and you're writing your episode, there is no supervising producer.

Yes, it's hard. Maybe they'll break a Margaret storyline in the room and I won't be there. But this is a show that has a little more time built into its schedule. In a network show you just miss it and that's it. This show, we go back over these outlines many, many times.

So you guys who write and produce, you never talk directly with HBO. What about network shows?

On a network show you have to get notes from the studio and then you get notes from the network. It's a killer. It destroys so much. And usually the studio notes are just brutal. Because they want to turn it out, they want to make everything about logic but writing is not about logic. Writing is about story. And often the people in the studio are not trained in story. Whereas I find people at the network have much more story under the belt. People at the studio – it's tough to get something out of there which is still good by the time you've taken their notes. But as a writer you do not get to meet these people. HBO believes in staying out of the show creatively. So does Showtime. Terry talks to HBO and that's it.

Why do you think there are so few women in TV and so few women showrunners?

Women in the United States make less than men.

Not only in the United States.

And it doesn't seem to be a point of concern to people in power. Until women object in a big way, it will not change. What is interesting is that some of the very best showrunners are women. Like Carol Mendelssohn, probably the best showrunner ever. She does *CSI*. She is absolutely spectacular. Shonda Rhimes is running three shows. They are unstoppable. The networks know that women make good showrunners because women want everybody to get along, they put out fires. It's a female thing where on a show you take care of so many details, it's like running a house and being a mom. Those qualities really translate to being a showrunner. I mean, really well. It's a small but extremely talented group. The hard part is getting women through the writers' room to move up the ranks, this is where I think the stop is. Women don't seem to get past the level of supervising producer. I personally haven't been on staff before, so this is great for me, but from what I've seen, women all seem to stop at supervising producer.

Why do you think that is?

They aren't allowed to go higher, not by women but by men. In the studies of the WGA and Equal Opportunity Employment, it is clear that there is just this ceiling. Writers' rooms are very uncanny, very cutthroat. So that is not necessarily an environment where women thrive. It is very male competitive. Women don't speak up in a way that can be heard by guys. People like Nina Tassler at CBS have a lot of female showrunners. Fox, NBC do not have a lot of woman showrunners, ABC yes. So it's also the network. But it's a funny thing because the majority of people that watch TV are female. For me it was clear right from the beginning I was never gonna rise to the ranks in a writers' room. I would never make it through a writers' room.

Why do you think that women do not speak up in a writers' room?

Whoever talks the loudest gets the most. So it's real hard when men compete with one another in the writers' room to break in. It can be very hard. It gets really tough and then they feel like, I don't know how to speak up and this person isn't listening to my ideas and it can get really gummy and then there's also just the tone of writing … You know, it's so funny, I feel like female stories get diminished by the media and critics, and male stories get celebrated. So a show can get super ratings and be about women but you know, a show like *Mad Men* is gonna get all the critics' attention. Because critics, and female critics as well, seem to like the male shows more. It's also in the world of TV criticism, if you read American critics, even American female critics, they are pretty tough on women writers in shows. And I don't want to be too general…And I don't think of myself as a male or female writer. I am a writer. But it's not very hard to help someone, is it? I'm over one hump.

Margaret, you started as an actress. Do you find this helpful when writing?

Yes, there are so many actors who write for TV now. Acting teaches you so much about writing and that is why actors make such good writers. I always say to writers, you should take an acting class. When you're an actor you study the human mind and behavior. Structure I had to learn but I always write from character. I do not think in story, I think in character. It's a strength but it can be also a weakness. Because I'm an actor I'm very well spoken, very articulate. So when I pitch, I can help them see it, I can almost dramatize it. It is tremendously helpful because I'm not afraid to speak to big scary people. It is so much scarier to audition than to pitch or defend an idea. Winnie Holzman[1] always says you should think of yourself as a writer. Just ignore all of that. Don't sacrifice anything. But think of yourself as a writer first.

So where do you want to go from here? What is your big dream?

I don't know. I like the camaraderie of television. I like being on the schedule and knowing we're gonna get something done by the end of the day. Movies can take years to make. I have a movie now that the studio has been having me write and rewrite for four years. And that's painful. And maybe it will get made. I'm also in a program right now. Ron Howard and Alliance hired nine writers to be like a Brain Trust. To develop new material for films for them because they thought that they were really stuck in terms of their development. So I'm also reading movies and giving notes on film scripts and rewriting a movie of my own for Ron, and I'm ... I'm too busy working to think of too much further than what my deadlines are. I mean, I want to write movies. But after a year alone at home writing a movie, I want to go work on a TV show. I'm an extroverted person and I like getting out and seeing people. That's the drawback of writing features. When the Writers Guild was thinking of striking we had this big meeting downtown and one side of the room was all the people who had written for television shows and they all knew each other and they were all friends and the other side were all the feature writers, they were all just sitting there, no one knows anybody. I don't know that I want to be locked in a room all the time. See, if I can produce my own movies then that would make me really happy. I am a producer on this movie that I've been writing for four years.

Would you like to direct?

Let me just get my kids through college (laughs).

Susan Miller

Susan Miller was a consulting producer/writer on Showtime's *The L Word* and ABC's *Thirtysomething*, as well as CBS' *The Trials of Rosie O'Neill*. She is executive producer/writer of the WGA award-winning web series *Anyone But Me*. She is also winner of two Obies, a Guggenheim Fellowship in playwriting and the Susan Smith Blackburn Prize for her plays *My Left Breast* and *A Map of Doubt and Rescue*.

You received the first WGA award ever for a web series. This is huge, right?

It means so much. To be the first. To be women receiving it. To be receiving it for a drama. A drama in which the two main characters are gay. Yeah. Huge.

How many fans do you have?

After three seasons, we have around 20 million views. With fans all over the world.

You started writing for TV as early as 1976 with Family, *and I saw you wrote for* Dynasty, *then for a show that was considered very innovative back then,* Thirtysomething.

Thirtysomething was a relationship-driven drama, groundbreaking at the time. The work I got in television was largely because I was a playwright. *Family* was conceived by Jay Presson Allen, who was also a playwright. Lucky for me, it was a time when Hollywood was attracted to writers who came from theater. Which is fortunately happening again. How I ended up writing for TV and film is one of those "small town girl gets discovered" stories. The Mark Taper Forum was producing one of my plays. My son was just a baby and when I separated from my husband, I decided to move to L.A. from Pennsylvania. So I went to a literary agency for representation. And I was in an agent's office talking about how I hadn't done anything for movies or television, and in walks a gorgeous young woman, also an agent, and she's complaining about her secretary. It turns out she's Kitty Hawks, daughter of famous filmmaker Howard Hawks. We're introduced and I say, listen, I came here to look for an agent but I can type, so if you decide to fire your secretary, I'm there. She called me a day later. I worked as her secretary for six weeks, until she got me my very first writing gig, replaced me with a new secretary, and became my agent. That was it. Six weeks later she was representing me.

That is some story.

(laughs) Yes. So I used the film and television work as grant money for writing plays. I was at the beginning of my playwriting career, so I would go back and forth to New York. I had plays done at the Public Theater (Joseph Papp was my mentor), Second Stage, and I became playwright in residence at The Taper with A Rockefeller Grant. I know my path wasn't conventional. You know, it's great you have your foot in the door, but you can get trapped. You have a choice to make. Security? Or taking risks by doing what you feel you're meant to do.

Many playwrights start working for TV and they never go back to the theater. But you have not worked for TV between 1997 and 2004.

I was writing movies in that period. At the same time I was doing a play in New York. I sold four original screenplays in a row. To Fox, Universal, Disney, Warner Brothers – on one pitch! That's a pretty rare thing. But they were never produced. The thing about screenplays is you can write and live anywhere. As opposed to television where you have to be in a room with the other creators. It's a writer-centric medium, which is why I love it. The best of television is like a novel. You have episodes like chapters, you can grow the characters, and there is scope to the stories. And I think American television has grown with the advent of cable. While American...I won't say cinema...American *movies* rely much more on proven formulas and the presence of celebrity.

Thirtysomething *was pretty groundbreaking at the time. Was it done with a writers' room?*

I've been on the staff of four television shows. And there was always a writers' room. *Thirtysomething* was Marshall Herskovitz and Ed Zwick's baby. There were only two or three writers on staff. We broke some stories together and would come up with episode ideas of our own. I was there for the inaugural season. The first season is always exciting but there's also a sense of, what is the style going to be, what are the dreams the creators have for the show and are you going to be able to contribute your own voice?

What do you think is the secret of success of American TV?

I think its success comes from show creators and writers who are given the power to express and stay true to their vision. The best work comes from original voices and demanding stories which don't sacrifice character. And this happens when writers are free to construct a world no one else could have imagined.

Did you have a writers' room on Anyone But Me?

It's just Tina (Cesa Ward) and me. At my dining room table or a coffee shop. So we sit down and discuss where we want the characters to go. We kind of outline, not to the point that it constrains us but just so we have a blueprint. And then we decide which episodes each one of us is going to write and the ones we'll write together, which we do by assigning scenes or parts of the story.

On IMDb Anyone But Me *is mentioned as a TV series.*

It's web TV. We're an indie web TV series, distributed and shown through the internet.

So how does it work? Who finances a web series?

Well, when we started this, I had that question too. Where is the money coming from to do this? When web series started out, a lot of them were done on handheld video camera, very low budget. With deferred payment to the crew and actors. We started this by paying people because we wanted to take our show to a different level and do it professionally. When I write for *Anyone But Me*, I'm putting as much into it as with anything else I write. It doesn't matter what size the screen is that people watch on; it doesn't matter if it's on a stage or not on a stage. We're breaking new ground, which is what I love.

How long are the episodes?

We do ten episodes per season and our episodes run somewhere between eight and 12 minutes. We try to keep them short because every page costs. The only episodes that are somewhat longer are usually the first and the last episode of each season.

So the length is determined by budget?

The budget determines it to a large degree. The story we want to tell also dictates the length. When I got into this, I called Marshall Herskovitz, one of the *Thirtysomething* creators, who was also working on a web series, the only one I had ever heard of – *Quarterlife*. I wanted to know what *is* this new world of web series? And the first thing he said was: "Don't do anything over ten minutes!" In a way it's good to have that condition because we started almost instinctively to be economical about what we wanted to say and how the characters say it. It's a unique challenge I like. Because you cannot waste time.

Is it also a matter of the attention span of the audience, as some people say?

That's changing. The medium up until now suggested that scripted content should be on the short side. Some web series air episodes of only 3–4 minutes. But we didn't want to do something so abbreviated. I think we're proof that people are willing and interested in seeing more fully developed versions of things. As the fans always tell us, "This should be longer!" You get into it and you want more. You get addicted. And we want people to go, "It can't be over now!"

So what is the budget?

It's grown, by necessity. We started at $6,000 for the first two episodes. And by Season Three that was doubled.

And that includes everything?

Well, Tina and I don't take writer or executive producer fees.

So you do it for the fun of it?

(laughs) I wouldn't say that. It *is* great fun. But it's the hardest work I've ever done. It's an all day, every day concern. Building an audience, growing a fan base, making a show. We have a company. And there's a long-term commitment. The best thing is you get the opportunity to work as an ensemble.

But you have to make a living.

I can afford to do this now so I'm doing it. But monetizing a web series is the biggest problem facing most creators.

Are you close to the break-even point?

Not yet.

So who is funding this?

We have an independent funder, who, after we launched the series, knew it had to build momentum. This commitment to being in it for the long haul is where we succeeded in relation to a lot of other web series that failed or never aired anything past a few episodes because they either didn't see the bigger picture or they weren't in it for the same reasons that we were. During the Writers' Guild strike, for instance, a lot of writers did something short for the web, but when the strike was over, they went back to doing what they usually do. Whereas we didn't see *Anyone But Me* as a *sample* to land a job somewhere else. We really put everything into the show itself, and that's the only way you can do it. I mean, television is different in that there is big money behind it. As a TV writer you don't have to go out and sell the show. As the writer/creator of a web series you are selling all the time. And wearing a lot of hats.

Don't the advertisers come to you? You've been on for three years now and that in itself is an achievement.

Advertisers have been pretty much web averse. A lot of series have donate buttons on their websites so fans can help out. And crowdsourcing sites like Kickstarter and IndieGogo have begun to do really well. But, we decided that we were going to do something nobody else had done. Kind of what PBS does. We were going to give the fans, the audience, a WebAThon. 90 minutes of totally new video on three separate nights. We had a hilarious video of the actors playing *Anyone But Me* charades. We hired a host and shot her doing an *Anyone But Me* walking tour all around New York to the various locations where we'd shot the show. We had interviews with the actors. And we had an eBay auction as well. It was a tremendous amount of work and we did ask people to support the show, but we were giving them something huge in return. We raised $32,000, which helped to fund our third season.

Who does all the networking and the social media management? I mean, this is as important as production for this type of production, right?

We do. I am constantly engaging the audience and making myself and the show known to the press. It's probably the most important and most time-consuming part of producing a web series.

So you do that yourself as well?

From the beginning. I just had to pursue every possibility. Not the least of which was finding a site to air the show. It's only by being open and reaching out to people that I found Strike TV, where we launched *Anyone But Me*. Then Tina and I went to a panel at the New School on Media Studies and heard about BlipTV – these are all distribution sites. So we introduced ourselves and went to their offices and became part of their lineup of original web series. The same with YouTube and Hulu, where we are now partners.

So you have different sites and you have your own site as well? And it's not like on TV, where your show it at one place exclusively, at least in the beginning?

We have our own website, but we're distributed non-exclusively on the other sites. And we get a revenue share from their ads. It's not much, but it helps. And these sites are essential for exposing the show. For instance, BlipTV featured us a lot on their home page. YouTube has done that as well, which is big. We had 80,000 views one day just because YouTube had it on their front page rollout.

Is it a kick to have a lot of views?

Oh my God, YES! YES! The first day, the day we launched, I happened to be in Minneapolis at the Playwrights' Center workshopping a play. Very nervous that no one would watch the show. But, we got 500 views that day and we were thrilled. Now, when we air a new episode, it's more like 30,000 views. And yeah, you get addicted to that, if you wanna know.

There is something special about the web series community. You get the impression of an incredible generosity and support among peers.

Yes! It's true. We're all trying to make a home in this new space. And we're in it together.

This is different from traditional media, where it is all about safeguarding. Do you think there is less competition?

I'm not saying that there isn't a competitive aspect to the web. Come on! But, we don't have a structure in place to protect, so we huddle together. There is a lot of fear in traditional media.

The fear that if one passes on something to someone else, one could miss out on something?

Yeah, we don't have that here.

There are no gatekeepers in web TV. But are you really free creatively? Doesn't the audience's reaction still define what you do?

Of course not! We don't ask people for their opinion about what we're writing! We don't take notes from the audience! On TV it's a joke how many notes you get and from whom. You're working with this production company, that production company, then this studio, then the network. My son is in this business too and I can step back and see what he has to go through, especially when he writes a pilot. Of course there are some very few people, like David Chase or David Kelley or perhaps David Simon, who can do whatever they want. Most TV writers, though, answer to a chain of people who answer to other people who ultimately answer to corporations. What makes what we're doing here unique is the autonomy. And the instant feedback we get from fans. Which is a lot like theater. It can get very heady. We're all making our own rules.

You are pioneers. It is surely exciting to be able to get immediate feedback from the audience.

I see them as the chorus, you know, our fans on Twitter and Facebook. They participate, it's communal, but we don't invite them to tell us how the story should go. We do love when they take sides with some of the characters. That's passion, that's great!

Is there room for narrative experiments?

Always. And that's so important. No one is going to make me adhere to a given formula. There's real creative freedom. That's why I'm doing this.

Well, you have the limits of your budget.

Sure.

I know that some people use this as an entry point to get to the real stuff. Is part of the dream inevitably that one of the networks knocks on your door?

We're not out there pitching. I mean, I've pitched features and television pilots. I know those rooms well. My old agent used to call me Sandra Koufax, you know as in Sandy Koufax the baseball pitcher? I had success, but I'm not interested in developing things old style. If someone comes to us and makes an offer, of course we'd consider it. But it's not a goal.

You think they're watching?

I don't know who's watching because there is so much to watch. But I do think TV execs are *aware* of us. And sure, I'd be happier if we did not have to struggle with raising the money ourselves. Of course I would. But I love being at the forefront here. Even with all the pitfalls of being at the forefront. To be ahead of your time is not always to your advantage, but what are you gonna do?

There's people who say this is going to be big in a few years and there are the skeptics who say that this is never gonna happen because it hasn't happened yet.

You know, I believe that all the arts can coexist. That they can inform one another and that they can also contribute to one another. That's what I believe. I can't predict if one will take over another. I hope not. I definitely think that we are earning a place at the table. Working in new media is becoming something that more people want to get involved in, more talented people, more serious people.

Are you union?

Our show is Writers Guild and some of the actors are SAG [Screen Actors Guild].

What do you shoot on?

We have shot different seasons on different formats. It depends on our DP.

Where does your audience come from?

We have a large international fan base. The UK is big, Germany is big, the Netherlands, France, China, South America, Canada.

How much of your audience is American?

Most of our viewers.

Do you think that is because of the lack of subtitles?

Not really. We have closed captioning now on all of our episodes that air on YouTube. And there's a function that allows anyone to make subtitles from that. I think because we're a New York show, it stands to reason we'd be most popular in the US.

How old is your audience?

From 16 to 40. Mostly in their 20s and 30s though.

What about other web series? Are you following what is out there?

When I'm writing I don't want to see other stuff. I don't want other stuff to be coming in. I need to stay focused. But, generally I try to see as many shows as possible, And now that I'm on the board of the IAWTV, at award time, all members have to watch every show that's submitted. So I'm pretty up to date. I think the quality of the work is definitely improving. And there are so many newcomers to the space. Which is a good sign.

Is Anyone But Me *now history?*

We aired our series finale in May 2012.

Did you always have an ending in mind?

I always had something in mind. But when we actually got to the point of ending the show, we kept it open-ended. Nothing is neatly resolved.

Like life.

Like life. I have another web series, a branded web series called *Bestsellers*. We made eight episodes. I created it and wrote it. Tina Cesa Ward directed it. Very different from *Anyone But Me*. It's about five women of different generations dealing with the conflicts of work and personal life who meet in a book club. I was hired to write it.

Who hired you?

CJP media and SFN.

Why did they fund this?

They wanted something that represented the aims of their company. There is a trend now towards branded web series which goes beyond product placement. The actors aren't holding up a box of cereal. In the case of Bestsellers, the sponsor doesn't have a product. They have a service. They place people in jobs. Their brand name only appears at the beginning of the episode. Otherwise, there is no plugging or compromise to the show itself.

Still, it's advertising.

Well, that's what branding a web series means. And actually in this case, it's been a great thing. Because I wasn't restricted in the content. The sponsor had practically no notes whatsoever. All they wanted was something that would represent the spectrum of employment they get for people. So I came up with a character who is an entrepreneur but has sold her company and now she is floundering. There's a character who is an executive travel advisor, a millennial who likes to work out of coffee shops. And a former ad executive who's now a Mommy Blogger, working from home. The budget of this show is absorbed by the sponsor. So I don't have to promote it in the way that I do with *Anyone But Me*. So far indie web series absolutely demand that the creators have to do all the work.

I guess the question is can you make a living from it, in the future if not right away?

I don't think there are many people who can afford to give up their day job to do just this, not yet. I'm hopeful there will be a paycheck someday. That the making of a web series will be supported. The question is always why we do what we do. And that question is always deeply personal.

Is there a system, an establishment which is emerging here?

There's no system in place that mimics traditional media where you submit your work to an agent and the agent submits it to an existing show, or submits your show to a network. It's a different kind of thing. It's about watching web series, seeing what has gotten attention. It's reading Tubefilter, the leading online new media journal. It's attending conferences and meetups. It's joining web series groups on Facebook. Or checking out the WGAE [Writers Guild of America East] digital caucus. It's taking part in determining the future of the space. And how to make your voice be heard in it.

You have explored similar storyworld ground with The L Word, *which was a TV series, as with* Anyone But Me. *And yet these two shows are very different.*

The L Word was set in L.A. And it concerned the lives of grown women in their 20s and 30s. By contrast, the backdrop for *Anyone But Me* is New York City, and our main characters are teenagers. Even though both series focus on gay relationships, stories about young people are going to have a different thrust. We wanted the characters on *Anyone But Me* to be attractive, but real. And we took care to handle their budding sexuality with passion yet restraint. There was an intentional glamour to *The L Word*. It dared to say, through its casting of beautiful women (who were also good actors), that lesbians are as cinematically sexy and fantasy-inducing as heterosexuals, who, as depicted in TV and film, are also almost always cast with beautiful women. *The L Word* had something to prove. And sometimes, in later seasons, it went too far. But, if you accept it as entertainment, it often hit the mark, and it created a world for people who had never had a world for themselves before.

Can you compare these two experiences for you as a writer?

I was a consulting producer/writer on the first season. I'm proud of what we achieved that year. There are a lot of people to satisfy when you're doing a television series for a major cable network like Showtime. And as the seasons keep going, it's a real balancing act to come up with new ideas and remain true to your vision. On the web we have sole ownership. It's up to us to stay on track, to hew to our own standards. We don't have to answer to anyone but ourselves and the fans. We aren't up against the same challenges that face creators of traditional corporate TV series. We're truly independent. To give you an example, with *Anyone But Me* when the actors who play our two main leads auditioned for their roles, we fell in love with them. Nobody told us we had to.

Reflections

In American TV drama the important component was and is the writer – so in order to be able to decipher TV drama's artistic and commercial success one must understand the writer and the way he or she creates. Illuminating the complicated creative process of an American TV show from as many different perspectives as possible was my main concern in this book, and it has been an educational and highly inspiring process.

American TV is said to be a writers' paradise, and this book has attempted to have a close look into that paradise but also to test the myth of absolute creative freedom. How is the writer's role defined in television and what are the main differences from a screenwriter's role in the film industry? How collaborative is the writing process of modern-day TV writing? Does the attendant idea that audiovisual storytelling can only result from the mind of a single genius still hold? How important is the writer's presence on set and during the whole process? One thing is certain – each show is different and each writer uses a different way to create it or to collaborate. The writers I spoke with often had very different answers to the very same questions. It is most interesting to see how each show is run differently, and how broad the spectrum of TV creating actually is. But even more interesting is to see the patterns emerging in conversation after conversation and the striking similarities between the different approaches, as well as the larger themes which are coming through. Let us now look at them, one by one.

The right men for the job

In the second episode of Season One of *Mad Men,* one of the copywriters is showing the agency to a new secretary, trying to impress her: "You

153

know...there are women copywriters!" he claims. – "Good ones?" – "Sure," he says. "I mean, you can always tell when a woman is writing copy. But sometimes she may be the right man for the job, you know?"

Not much has changed since the days depicted in *Mad Men*. Or at least, not enough. This is still a man's world, and sometimes a woman will get a writing job not because she is "the right man for the job" but because she is a woman. As Jenny Bicks puts it, in the writers' rooms she has worked in it was usually herself "and a bunch of guys" and "it still is that way." In the conversations this is one of the topics that kept coming up, together with the fact that there are so very few African-American or Hispanic or Asian writers. American TV is written for the most part by white men.

In terms of the writer's sensibility it would surely be naïve to say that gender doesn't influence how you see the world and how the world sees you. But how does the fact that we, the audience are being told stories coming from the worldview of a certain limited population group influence our own sense of reality and worldview? And how does that sense of reality turn us into an audience that wants more of what it is used to getting?

These are fascinating questions in themselves. In the context of this book, however, it seems more appropriate to look at how American TV is written, because of the white male predominance among writers. And while doing so I will concentrate on the gender issue, notwithstanding the fact that this is also a race issue and an age issue – and all the reflections below can be applied in relation to all these issues too.

Margaret Nagle makes an interesting point when she talks about how the function of the writers' room is geared towards typically male competitiveness and how the framework (studios, critics, etc.) has a built-in disadvantage for women and women's stories. Warren Leight makes the same point, warning of the dangers of "a certain kind of alpha male personality that can destroy a writers' room." "That guy can ruin the room," he says. This is, of course, a most fascinating aspect of collaboration: that it can hold competition, either open or hidden. A writers' room is like a classroom. The students will compete for the teacher's approval, as well as for the best grades. And some students will be more competitive than others. Is this a gender issue? Are men more competitive than women? Is it a matter of leadership? Is it a matter of education?

And why are there fewer women than men writers in the rooms? As Diana Son points out, cultural and social context can affect who is able or encouraged to pursue a writing career in the first place. "You have to consider first who says, I want to be a writer," she says. "You know it's a long shot. You know that the chances of you being successful are slim. And that you're going to spend years toiling away with no reward until someone 'discovers' you. So, not a lot of people can afford to do that. It's a cultural thing."

But surely there are enough women writers out there? Film schools are producing a new wave of women writers every year, and it does feel like there are many women writers around – but so very few at the top.

Margaret Nagle makes the point that in her opinion some of the very best showrunners are women – like Carol Mendelssohn, who runs *CSI*, or Shonda Rhimes, who is running three shows at the moment. Nagle thinks that "the networks know that women make good showrunners, because women want everybody to get along, they put out fires." For her, taking care of so many details on a show is "like running a house and being a mom," so a traditionally female thing. The parent analogy is also made by Janet Leahy, who says that as a showrunner "you have to make sure people are taken care of and that they don't receive the stress you're receiving." Jenny Bicks explains why women are in her opinion better suited to be showrunners than men: "I think we have an ability to multitask. They've done all these tests on men's brains, which show that they are capable to compartmentalize – but we are better diplomats, we hear people." And still, it is hard getting women through the writers' room to move up the ranks, which is where most see the stop. Women don't seem to get past the level of supervising producer very easily.

But why is that? If everybody agrees that the female personality is the best fit for the showrunner job description, as Margaret Nagle points out, then why is the reality so very different?

It looks as if the answer is to be found in perception, as well as in our system of perception. Nagle is not the only one who feels that female stories get diminished by the media and critics, and male stories get celebrated. In fact a lot has been written about this, also in relation to the show *Girls* created by Lena Dunham, the youngest woman showrunner around. There's a tiny aperture for women's stories – and a presumption that men won't watch them.[1] It seems that critics, including female critics, almost like the male shows more, or somehow find them more discussable. (*Girls* is, of course, also discussed a lot, but more as a cultural phenomenon than as a show in its own right. In fact it spawned an intense and frenzied debate about feminism and gender politics.)

Perception does not only happen at the level of a produced series. It also happens in its genesis. As Diana Son points out, one has to consider who is making the hiring decisions. "What are they responding to when they read a writer's work? Most execs and showrunners are white men and you know, we all respond to work that feels familiar to us. Comfortable. Whether we know it or not. There's a shared aesthetic, a shared interest or sense of humor." This sounds like a never-ending cycle, and most probably that is exactly what it is. "As long as white men are making the decisions then the majority of people they hire are going to be people who feel familiar to them." Janet Leahy tends to agree: "Traditionally, I think it's been because men like working with people they know and feel comfortable with, and that's usually other men." And yes, "there is just a lot of discrimination in this business. There's a great deal of age discrimination as well. I have a lot of friends who are out of work because they're over 40."

Although the men writers I talked with have naturally not thought about this as much as the women writers, the general consensus across the board was that the rooms are indeed too white and too male. However, most seemed to feel that this was changing for the better. Perhaps it is changing because fewer and fewer women allow the state of things to discourage them. As Janet Leahy points out, this business is transforming every day and opportunities are shifting constantly. And ultimately, one can buy into the discrimination, or one can create one's own opportunities.

No one tells the writers what to do

"You figured the place out yet?" – "What do you mean?" – "How it runs." – "I know the copywriters tell the art department what to do and I know the account executives tell the copywriters what to do." – "What?! No one tells the writers what to do except for the head of creative, your boss, Don Draper. Don't think because he's good-looking he's not a writer!"

Although this dialogue from the second episode of Season One of *Mad Men* probably represents the predominant idea that in TV writers call the shots, the reality, in most cases and with very few exceptions, is that of course someone tells the writers what to do. For one thing someone tells Don Draper, the equivalent of a showrunner, what to do. "Quality TV" is still part of our permission-based culture; only extraordinary continuous success leads sometimes to absolute creative freedom. How, when and to what extent is an important part of the conversations held in this volume.

For the first time in history a writer/screenwriter has real creative rights and power: she can have a vision and follow it through; a project can be funded on the basis of the writer's name, and critics, scholars, funders and the audience know who she is. This writer is called a showrunner.

Perhaps the best description of a showrunner is given by Margaret Nagle when she describes Terence Winter, in whose room she was when I talked with her: "It's all about his taste, point of view, his voice, his eye, he's the architect of this great, big beautiful house with many rooms." As a writer in the room she may decorate the kitchen but ultimately what prevails is the showrunner's vision of how the kitchen should look, what materials should be used and how it should be connected to the other rooms. The showrunner's vision applies not only to story, but also to the look of the show. As Terence Winter points out: "There's a certain world depicted, at least that's my philosophy, and it should look like the same place every week."

Perhaps the most extreme example of what a showrunner's clout may mean is given by Janet Leahy, discussing David Kelley and *Boston Legal*: "We rarely received notes from the studio or network because of David's clout," she says. "Our draft would go up to David, he would call with his notes. The other executive producer Bill D'Elia gave his notes and we'd do our rewrites. Occasionally the network called with a note, but it couldn't be more than three or four times. We had a lot of freedom to do what we wanted."

This is rarely the case, though. And it is definitely more challenging in a network environment. Says Eric Overmyer: "Network executives want everything explained, they want to simplify everything, and you often get that feeling that the draft gets weaker and weaker. That's commonplace. Studios are dealing by fear, they're afraid of sponsors, they anticipate, and make sure that disasters don't happen. There's a lot of people whose job is to give notes. You get endless notes, making it more palatable, less spicy, more melodramatic, more like what has been done before." He makes a point of clarifying that this is not the same with HBO: "They try to understand what's happening there; it is a creative approach." As Robert Carlock puts it, very diplomatically: "Good executives are better than bad executives."

Writing for TV is probably the toughest writing there is; the pressure is enormous and to be creative under such pressure is in itself a major achievement. Being a showrunner, leading the writers who write a show with you, is a high-pressure job on every level. You have to be enormously resourceful, quick and decisive, and you're constantly managing and creating at the same time. Let us look at some of the challenges, and first of all at how a showrunner casts and runs a room.

A bigger brain

The prevailing idea is that film, like any other art form, is made by a single genius. TV drama is, however, more often than not the result of collaboration between many writers and minds. How is that possible, and what does it mean?

First of all, one has to say that although there are also cases where the writers are working as freelance writers without really ever sitting down with all the other writers of the season, the room seems to be the one element which defines the process and which is here to stay – although there is also a consensus that the tendency is for the rooms to get smaller.

But what is the room? And how did it come into being?

Writers' rooms already existed back in the 1950s, when three or four of the old comic legends would hang out and try out their jokes and material. The writers' room concept has evolved through time. In the 1980s and 1990s the rooms grew bigger, you went from having three or four writers in a room to 15 writers. Today, due to budget limitations, the rooms have started getting smaller again. Whether it's a large group of comedians trying to one-up one another with jokes on a sitcom or writers being assigned specific episodes after a small group of writers has "beat out" the storyline together, what is important is the physical presence of the writers in one space – thus "room."

As Warren Leight says, the room is smarter than the individual. It's a bigger brain. Still, and although the predominant idea is that American TV is produced in writers' rooms and that the writers' room model is directly linked to good TV writing, the conversations showed that not all showrunners are friends of the room concept. And where there is a room, the way it is run is in no way pre-defined or canonical. Almost each room seems to work a bit differently from any other, depending on who the showrunner is and how she likes to run it.

The next question is then, does it make it easier if there is a writers' room? For some shows one has to produce 51–52 pages for 45 minutes and once the writer has a beat sheet which summarizes everything in 19–20 pages, it usually takes her 1–2 weeks to write an episode. Then there are notes, a second draft, a read-through with the actors. If the whole process goes through the room, doesn't that slow it down? Or does it make it easier? The more the merrier; but if we are going to use proverbs, don't too many cooks also spoil the broth? And isn't it more time-consuming as a whole?

The time aspect is indeed the main reason why some showrunners dislike the room concept. For instance, a successful procedural like *Law & Order* will not have a writers' room in the classic sense of the word. Warren Leight explains that this is because a group cannot plot that tightly. Then there is the other extreme. I have often heard the story of two or more writers' rooms working in parallel, in competition against each other for the best script of the same episode of one show or another.

So what exactly happens in the room? Tom Fontana is one of the showrunners who is not particularly enthralled by the concept, so he is naturally rather critical when he describes a day in the room: "In most writers' rooms, everyone comes in at nine o'clock to break stories, but out of eight hours, you spend at least an hour and a half eating, you spend at least two hours talking about your life, an hour on your cell, and so the actual amount of time that the necessary work gets done, is a relatively small part of a very long day." Which is why for his shows the writers get together but not in a "let's sit around and write stories" way. What works for him is to sit down one on one with the writer who's going to write an episode and work with her on that episode.

Of course this is not how any other showrunner who finds the writers' room a useful concept would describe it. Still, running a room means leading a group of people and that can prove strenuous. Whoever gives guidance to the room will try to reach consensus about directions on stories, because someone has to lay out the storyline, whether through reasoning or by simple taste. Someone has to be the filter because otherwise the writers will just go on talking. Someone has to steer the ship.

Which means that naturally hierarchy defines this world of synergy and collaboration and creative freedom. In Robert Carlock's words: "There's a hierarchy of seniority: there's certain people who will take a room (give guidance to the room), certain people who are learning to take a room and people who are staff writers." Actually, starting from the top, the hierarchy goes from executive producer to co-executive to supervising producer to producer, co-producer, and then down to executive story editor, story editor and staff writer. Depending on what the issue is at hand, the room can be led by different people, but the final word always belongs to the showrunner.

As the above-mentioned titles show, a TV writer's job is not just about writing. Part of her job is producing – she'll go to casting, she'll take part in creative meetings, she'll be on set. Again, this is not always the case, and the producers' titles depict first and foremost the hierarchy in the writing staff. It's a way to delineate the level at which you are functioning – it's like ranks in the military, from private to general. It's a raise in pay and a raise in responsibility; it's an acknowledgment of the fact that you've been in the business for a long time and that you have more of a track record. There are, however, co-executive producers who are really doing what most people would consider the nuts and bolts of producing, which is what things cost and how much time it will take, and juggling the things that the writers want with what is actually practical, while at the same time dealing with the network and the studio. Beyond all that, their job is creative. A showrunner's job is primarily to make sure that the scripts are produced on time and in the best possible quality – and to run the show according to these scripts, to follow through with the show's vision.

Jenny Bicks speaks about how she ran the room at *Sex and the City*, implementing what they called the "independent study," whereby each writer would take care of her own episode, from start to finish. She would leave the room and write an outline, after it was broken down – an outline scene by scene, describing what happens in each scene. Then (as a showrunner) Jenny would take the outline back into the room, she would take comments from the room and then give notes to the writer about what she thought they should address. The writer would again go away, write their script and the same thing would happen: a script would come back into the room, everybody would read it, give notes, and then the writer would make the changes which the showrunner decided upon – and only then would it go to the studio and then to the network.

Which highlights the next question: how great is the danger that working with a room and trying to reach consensus will lead to the lowest common denominator? One would expect it to be very great; however, the results seem to imply that the opposite is the case. Can it be that a group is ultimately more courageous in breaking ground, in challenging preconceptions, in going places one has never visited before?

Musical chairs

One of the topics that stood out was the way a showrunner picks the writers for the room, the way she "casts" the room. Warren Leight talked about looking for a cultural mix and finding people who have some connection to the experiences and backgrounds of the characters. Robert Carlock, on the other hand, for the type of shows he does, is looking for people who can write everybody. "Diversity is what you're looking for," he says.

Terence Winter, Warren Leight and Jenny Bicks all talked about the importance of having people that are willing to be open with the other writers, bare their soul and pitch in when needed. "What's really important to me," says Winter, is a willingness to open up about yourself, about your past, about things that have embarrassed you, weird stuff about yourself – you have to open up your veins and spill it out in the writers' room – because that's the stuff that we tell stories about. I would like to hear from you what's the most embarrassing thing that's ever happened to you.

Winter also talks about what he calls "hangability:" "If there's a person I want to hang out with every day, they are talented, they seem like they get the show, they have a good sense of humor, they don't seem crazy, if I can stay in the room with this person for ten hours a day, and not wanna strangle them ... " Then, that's his man. Or woman.

It is obvious that in the process writers will get typecast. This is a Catch-22. If you want to do something you haven't done before, chances are it will not be an easy task to persuade the decision makers to trust you – because you haven't done it before. And that's exactly why you should do it, of course. Doesn't being creative mean experimenting, doing new things, going against the usual way of doing things, risking, inventing? How can you do all these things when you have developed your habits, when you have become comfortable in your own ways?

In the same spirit, a showrunner will also go back to people she has worked with successfully in the past. Eric Overmyer makes it very clear: "If I were to start a show and I were allowed to hire a big staff, I might be able to come up with ten names – and they're all people I've worked with before. It's because I don't know other people. And because it's very risky taking a chance on somebody you don't know. It's a very closed system."

Not only that – you also have to get everybody approved. And then you might get to hear the fearful comment, which Overmyer talks about: "OK, you've done some independent features but you've never done an HBO show. You don't have the experience. But how do I get that experience, if you don't hire me?" Once you're in, you do well, asserts Overmyer. But it's hard to get in – and it seems harder and harder these days. It is indeed "like musical chairs, where the chairs get fewer (as the rooms get smaller) and they keep sending people in."

So how few are the chairs? What is the right size for a writers' room? Warren Leight says it is five writers. This means that everyone gets to speak, and that there aren't too many different directions. Robert Carlock describes the reasoning behind the size of the *30 Rock* writers' room: "Including Tina, I think we're 13 this year. At *Friends* it was between 12 and 14 in the few years I was there. What that number allows you to do, which is sort of crucial, is to split into two groups." These are the so-called ancillary groups, which are created to maximize the efficiency. So "one group may be working on a script which is shooting in two weeks and another group is working on creating the stories for the script after that."

When you like to hear your words

As Janet Leahy points out, people don't go to writing to be rewritten. But they still are, first and foremost by the showrunner. The showrunner is the writer who tells the writers what to do, and who will eventually do it herself.

So should a showrunner polish the final draft of every episode to preserve the "voice" of the series, or should each individual writer be allowed to use their voice to bring out new sides to the characters and the series? The conventional wisdom seems to come directly from auteur theory and wants everything to be from one mold, carrying a single signature and voice – so as to pretend that one person wrote it.

I was most intrigued by something Jenny Bicks said, when she talked about using different writers in *Sex and the City*. She explained how she will not rewrite physically but rather give notes to the writer as opposed to polishing the writer's draft herself. But then again, Bicks believes that a show works best if there is more than a singular voice, and if a different aspect of each character gets represented by each writer: "If you watch *Sex and the City*, you'll notice that each episode feels maybe a little different. I know which writer wrote it, because it is perhaps a bit more cynical, more of a cynical side of Miranda, more this kind of Carrie, and in the end it's the different characters but it's not one voice. It's one voice with different angles."

Most of the writers suggest that each writer gets a shot at two drafts before the showrunner comes in for a polish or sometimes a rewrite. Terence Winter makes a good point here: "I would hope that the writer at least gets me 50% there. Give me a draft, which is halfway to where I need it to be. Ideally it would be 95%. But when they miss the mark so completely that I need to rewrite it from the first page, then it's usually an indication that this is not gonna work."

A showrunner taking over is not always a bad thing. Charlie Rubin gives us a slightly different point of view when he talks about his experience with the showrunners of *Seinfeld*: "It tended to be that the more they liked it the quicker they took it," he says. "Though sometimes what they liked was the idea, not what you were doing with it," he adds in all honesty.

Very rarely, the second draft will get written in the room. Robert Carlock talks about how this will be done: "You project it (the screenplay) on the screen and you scroll through and if you're trying to fix a joke, you end up with a page and a half of possible jokes so you have to choose one, erase the others and put that one in. And that's usually 30–35 pages that you're rewriting. Then you take it to a table read."

But what does it mean for a writer to be writing in the show's voice, and so ultimately in someone else's voice? Diana Son uses the example of *Law & Order*, which she was writing for some time, and talks about how she would write a line and she would think that the showrunner was going to love it: "It sounds like a line he would write. And then, I'm in another scene, and I think, Oh my God, I am so tempted to write this line and I know that René will hate it, but to amuse myself I'm just gonna put it in. And then, after René rewrote me, I would find out that he rewrote the line I thought sounded just like him and he kept the line that was so me that I thought he wasn't going to like it."

So perhaps it is not about trying to write in the showrunner's voice? Perhaps it is more than that? As Tom Fontana says, as a showrunner he does not want to be handed back scenes which he could have written himself. After all, collaborative writing means that each one contributes what they are best at and what they are needed for: their individualism, their very own truth. Still, a writer is taking a risk every time she goes off track, and it may very well go wrong.

At least three of the writers I talked with stressed a single piece of advice: stay true to yourself. Don't chase fads or write what you think someone wants to see. Jane Espenson talks about "trusting your own instincts and your own good taste." Jenny Bicks encourages "writing what you want to write, going towards the love" and Tom Fontana very simply states that "being successful is being faithful to oneself."

Tom thinks that people often look to being successful as opposed to being faithful: "And when I say faithful, I mean faithful to themselves and to the truth within them. And I think it's very easy for that to get lost in the need to be successful, in the 'Oh, I want the trophies, I want the money, I want the car, I want the house' way. And I only say that having been seduced by that and then having woken up and said, 'Well, wait a minute, is that really what I wanted out of being a writer?'" Tom talks about how he probably could have had a more successful career and how there were several times when he chose to not do what was commercially the wisest choice. He feels like he has been continually faithful to his writing, though, and because of that, he doesn't feel the need to be successful in his career in a traditional way (although, of course, he is that, too).

Success is a relative thing anyway. Some of the shows we have been discussing here, had they been on one of the traditional networks, would have been canceled because the numbers would have been too low. It's one thing talking about three or four million people watching, and another if what you need is an audience of 15 million people, as is the case with network TV. And that concerns content and language too: the more people you're trying to please, the more the edges will become dull and disappear. This is surely another reason for the success of cable TV.

As said, distribution (and the evolving patterns of attention) is one of the systems which are under review, and is changing at this very moment anyway. Binge viewing is one of the new phenomena; another is the long afterlife of a show. *The Wire* is a good example – most people didn't watch it while it was running, in fact by the last season it had under a million viewers. But now it's a classic and it has had (and still has) a very long life on DVD. As our industry is changing, it looks as if we may need a longer time frame to be able to define real financial or artistic success.

An issue that is directly connected with the issue of rewriting is writing credit. If more than one writer is involved in the writing of one episode, who should be credited? Terence Winter makes it very clear that he considers rewriting, where necessary, part of his job as the showrunner and head writer, and that he is therefore not overly friendly toward the idea of taking credit for it – whoever was assigned the script initially, their name stays on it. "I'll only put my name on scripts that I write in their entirety from the beginning," he says. But obviously showrunners are split about this. There are showrunners who feel that if they rewrite more than 50% of a script, they should definitely be putting their name on it.

For Warren Leight there's no relationship between who writes what and how credit is determined in TV: "It's a very bad credit system we have. Obviously, in a writers' room system everyone is pitching in on everyone's episode and sometimes the only way justice can be done is to distribute credit evenly." Again, matters are in the hands of the showrunner. Warren explains how he will try to reward the people who work harder with a little more credit as the season goes on. "But there are people who only care about credit and that kills you," he adds.

Everyone who has rewritten someone else's screenplay knows how difficult it is not to change more rather than less and to not have the feeling that one has had to rewrite everything. Rewriting is a tricky business. On the one hand it is easier than writing because one does not have to face the blank page. On the other hand it needs a lot of sensibility and capability to be able to rewrite and not create a new draft – with its very own first draft problems.

Jane Espenson says it as clearly as possible: "As a writer, I like to hear my words. As a showrunner, I like to hear my words. So I probably rewrite a little more as a showrunner than writer-me would like." She adds: "It's not a bad or hurtful thing. The show is not there to give the writers a chance to hear their words. The writers are there to serve the show and the showrunner."

A better place for writers

Whether in TV or in the movies, if you look into the development process and how a screenplay is being developed and how many people have a say or a go, it's amazing that any lines get through from first draft to the screen. Still, TV is a better place for writers than any of the other dramatic media, with the sole exception of the theater, of course. Besides, TV drama is nowadays so highly regarded that it is already changing some of the old rules. The crossover of the boundary between cinema and TV, whereby writers can move once again from one medium to the other, with greater ease, is one of them. It remains to be seen whether the crossover experiment will eventually become a tradition and whether such tradition will affect the writer's importance in other media too.

In television, writer-producers write their own scripts and they rewrite other people's scripts; it's their show and their vision. In the movies, it's all about the director. As opposed to movies where the writer won't even be on set, in TV it is the writer who tells the director what to do. Tim Van Patten talks about the tone meeting from the point of view of the director. This is the meeting where the director sits down with the writer-producer and the writer of the episode, the line producer and the first AD and they run through the script and trade notes or suggestions. "On *Sopranos* that tone meeting would happen in the middle of your prep and the director called it 'defending your life,' because you would go in there and normally the writer would go through the script and you would sort of take notes and it was a lot of pressure. It was very stressful, because you had to say how you were going to approach the scene, what you thought it meant."

Clearly, in TV it is the director who feels the pressure and who has to pitch her approach. Will this change now that more and more feature film directors cross over to TV? Will they bring their mentality with them? Or will they be educated in a different way of working and eventually even bring it back to the movies, changing the predominant mentality there?

Surely the most difficult crossover for a writer is from the theater to the movies. Diana Son talks about the ultimate writer's shock: "You've been in the theater where you are the most important person in the world and no one is in that room unless the playwright is there...and you go to the cinema, where you are not even invited to the set ..." In TV even a staff writer goes on set – which is perhaps why TV has become the place where playwrights go to make a living. TV is a way for writers to have a relatively steady job with a decent income.

It may sound like a point of courtesy, even a detail, whether a writer is on set or not, but it is not. In fact it is one of the most important factors behind American TV drama's success, perhaps even more so than the writers' room concept. The fact that the writers are on set allows for better writing. Let us see how.

Terence Winter makes the point that good writing is writing which is changeable till the very end. Warren Leight talks about listening to the actors and their emotional evolution, and how the storylines should obey that instead of the storylines forcing the characters to do things that they are not yet ready for. The two concepts are related and they presuppose the presence of the writer on set and during the whole process. I will suggest that ultimately, it is that which makes for great writing and which is missing from the movies. When the writer is kept out of the process, the writing does not evolve – or evolves without the involvement of the person who has conceived of the story and the characters and who knows their finest nuances.

In the movies, and unless writer and director are one and the same person, the one person who has deep knowledge of the story is the one who cannot hear whether her lines are working, cannot see what is doing the job and what is not; and when the scene is on its feet, cannot delete or add anything. It is someone else who will do all that, if it is done at all – and all this happens in the name of some strange policy deriving from fearing the writer and excluding her from the process.

Tom Fontana goes further than that. For him, writers not being on set actually makes for bad writing: "In television, things happen so fast it's really important for a writer to be around and say, 'Now here's the intention of the scene.' If the writer does not participate actively, his instinct is to overwrite the scene and to make it very obvious what the scene is about. But that's the worst kind of writing, because it has no subtlety. That's what a writer needs to do when he's not on set, and that makes for bad TV."

Or for a bad feature film. Even if things do not happen as fast as in TV (which may not be true) every single word of the above remark is directly applicable to the movies – unless, of course, writer and director are one and the same person. And that is a very interesting thing to think about: could it be that the brilliance of many auteur films is ultimately based on the fact that the writer is on set (as she is also the director) and can therefore work further on the script once the scenes are on their feet, as we say? Could it be that auteur cinema is ultimately more about the way writing is being treated in its process than about anything else? Most professional screenwriters and TV writers will not invoke the sanctity of the screenplay as they have written it – but they will caution against the arbitrary disintegration of story and characters which happens when the original writer is not involved. In TV the original writer may indeed be rewritten during production, sometimes (rarely) even in her absence. But never in the absence of the showrunner, who is ultimately a writer more than anything else – a writer who was there when the story was conceived and who knows the characters' finest nuances.

Despite the writer-unfriendly environment, some TV writers have not given up entirely on the movies. "In America, cinema is even more difficult to get into as a writer than TV," says Eric Overmyer. "It's jealously guarded by the A-list writers who get a lot of money to do rewrites. I'd love to get some of that work too," he says. "It's hard to get. If I had more time I'd write a spec script."

Most writers, however, have had such bad feature film experiences that they often end up avoiding the movies. Terence Winter is very outspoken about the disrespect he felt from being rewritten by a film's director – an experience which is common in writers' circles, far too common and far too painful. Jenny Bicks's film also ended up far from where she initially intended when she was writing the script – and that is probably the second most talked-about issue in writers' circles, when one talks about movies. Is it even possible for someone else to improve on what a writer has in mind when she writes? Is to direct the only way to get what she has in mind on screen? And if so, is it true that writers make for bad directors? In our industry the legend goes that films from screenwriters are not good enough – how often does one hear "he/she should stick to writing"? And, by the way, how often does one hear "he/she should stick to directing"? Not nearly as often. Does this mean that writers have to deal with preconceptions, and that people expect them to fail when directing? Or that it is easier to direct than to write? Whatever the truth, whenever a writer sets off to direct she knows she will have to go against these preconceptions, and that they may have also found their way into her own mind – and that is, ultimately, more difficult to deal with.

Tom Fontana is very frank about his reasons for sticking to writing for TV: "To me, telling the story, exploring characters, defining the times we live – that's what it's about, and if I can do it on TV and have the freedom I get, why would I trade that to write a movie where I'm gonna be shit on because screenwriters are notoriously shit on by directors? What do I need it for? Also right now the movies that are being made … I don't have an interest in them."

Indeed, character drama seems to have migrated to television, perhaps together with the writers. And that is definitely another valid reason for sticking to TV, when that is why you started writing in the first place.

It is interesting to see that the writer's position in the movies is the one theme which all the writers in this book agree on and are also very passionate about. Says Jenny Bicks: "Generally writers are tossed aside. Whether it's good or bad, once you produced that thing it gets handed over to the director and it's the director who's the showrunner." So does it make a difference, I wonder, whether you are rewritten by a director or by a showrunner? Terence Winter says it does, most definitely. A showrunner, being first and foremost a writer, will ask questions, she will respect the writing. A director just rewrites, sometimes without even having the talk, often completely misunderstanding what is on the page.

The problematic relationship of writer and director is also the main reason Warren Leight prefers being in TV rather than in the movies. Plus the fact that he hates "wasting time waiting for something to get a green light. That's not time you get back." Indeed, a TV writer has a very different concept of time than a screenwriter. A screenwriter's life consists of a lot of time waiting – waiting for a green light, waiting in turnaround, waiting for a director to do his draft. In comparison a TV writer is constantly creating – under time pressure. In fact it makes you wonder how television's intensely pressurized production conditions – episodes penned by multiple writers and shot in a few days on relatively small budgets – does not creatively disadvantage the medium in relation to the movies. The range is, of course, extensive. A show like *Boardwalk Empire* will shoot in 12–15 days, a show like *In Treatment* will shoot in two days. Warren Leight speaks about the difference one shooting day can make in a show like *Lights Out* (which shot in seven days). "Network is eight, some cable is seven, HBO is a hundred." He exaggerates to make a point, but "seven shooting days is the norm now in a lot of basic cable, and it's tough." Of course this also influences the writing time. And still most TV writers "like being under that kind of gun." For one thing writing is what makes a writer happy, and a TV writer writes a lot.

How come that in TV when writers could also easily hire themselves to direct, as Tom Fontana makes very clear, they rarely do? Most of the writers answered humbly that the job of a TV director needs certain skills which they do not have; others that the tempo is so insane that it would be impossible to do both jobs. The highly collaborative high-pressure world of TV drama favors separation of skills.

Another reason for staying out of the movies is the infamous "fire and hire policy." Says Jenny Bicks: "Generally in movies it goes like that: Oh, we don't like this draft, well, let's hire another writer. Which I think is a mistake, not just ego-wise but also in terms of creating a singular voice." Perhaps that is one of the main reasons for the different personality TV writers seem to have when compared with screenwriters. For one thing, because of the rooms, TV is a much more sociable place. Margaret Nagle talks about the time when the Writers Guild was thinking of striking and "we had this big meeting downtown and one side of the room was all the people who had written for television shows and they all knew each other and they were all friends and the other side were all the feature writers, they were all just sitting there, no one knows anybody."

It is not only that they do not know each other. They are each other's fierce competition.

"When people ask me how do you break into TV, I say the secret is, on your very first show, try to have your office next to the guy who's going to create *Seinfeld*," jokes Charlie Rubin, who is actively educating a new generation of TV writers. As said, television is a very insular business, and also a very difficult business to penetrate, especially if you are coming from the outside. Most of the writers I talked with for this book turned out to be related in some way. Not related by blood, but related through belonging to some sort of "family." Bruce Paltrow's family, Tom Fontana's family... "Raised by Bruce," "he's one of Tom's kids" were expressions I heard often, and they are parent–child expressions. In fact Tom got his start from the late Bruce Paltrow and is now continuing the tradition – and he is not the only one.

Still, it would be wrong to forget that TV is also a very competitive place, and I cannot stop noticing the generosity theme that has come up. Are successful writers more relaxed and so share more information more easily? Do they have less difficulty with giving? Or are these qualities actually the ones that have made them so successful in the first place? Which came first, the chicken or the egg? In any case, there is clearly a correlation.

A matter of quantity

Thanks to all that is being reported about the writers' paradise and all the attention which American TV has received in the last ten to 15 years, more and more feature writers are now crossing into TV. "For a while it was us going to the movies," says Rubin, "now there are movie guys coming in and writing pilots." Everybody wants to have a taste of writers' paradise. Still, depending on where you are coming from, you may experience it as a quirky paradise.

Many of the TV writers I talked with have a theater or literature background. Eric Overmyer talks about the ego involved in the question of whose intellectual property it is: "When you're on staff on a television show you want to bring something to it and you want to make it better, but it doesn't belong to you." In theater or literature it does. Indeed, some of the writers seemed to have almost a bigger respect for the forms they had left behind and to which they were dreaming of returning one day – once making a living stopped being the priority. Susan Miller talks about how you can get trapped once you have your foot in the door in TV, and how at some point you have a choice to make if what you really want to do is write for the theater.

In that context, it is interesting to think about the influence one form of writing has or will have on another. TV has influenced cinematic narration and vice versa for many years now. But what about the theater? When so many playwrights are currently making a living by writing TV, an influence is sure to be seen. Charlie Rubin is convinced that playwrights will write better plays as a result of the time that they spent in TV. "They'll come back and they'll have learned all those kinds of lessons and they'll be able to afford to work for the theater. That's my prediction, somewhere around 2020 we're going to see an amazing flowering in the theater. I just feel it. It used to be fail in theater, fail in movies, go to TV. Now it'll be succeed in TV, succeed in theater."

Warren Leight also comes from the theater and is in fact a successful playwright, but he is not dreaming of going back. He focuses on the bright side of TV writing: "There is a joy in TV – I have more control of my storyline here, in some ways more than as a playwright. And it's hard to get a play made, it's just hard to get them up nowadays. While in four months I did 35 episodes of *In Treatment*, in four months at *Lights Out* we did 13 episodes, that's an awful lot of storytelling. You are lucky to get a play every three years in New York, you know, and the wait drives me crazy."

New kid on the block

So where does the newest of all media come in? What about the world-wide web? For the moment there is one form that seems to have prevailed and that is probably because it approximates an existing form – that of serialized TV. The web series consists of episodes that last anywhere from five to 15 minutes, and they are offered in the known dramatic unity of a season. In fact, IMDb, the industry's most used online database, lists web series as TV series.

What is the difference between a TV series and a web series, apart from length? How does length get defined? Can you actually tell a story in ten minutes? We have only vaguely touched upon all these questions in this book – especially in my conversations with Jane Espenson and Susan Miller, both experienced TV writers who are also writing for the new medium – as the medium is still in flux and obviously in that early phase when a new medium is mimicking another and is actually being used as a side door to the traditional media. For one thing, no writer can make a living from a web series. There is no funding system in place yet, not for a drama series. Yet still people make them.

Susan Miller reflects that it is probably the hardest work she's ever done: building an audience, growing a fan base, making a show, all at the same time – and you have to be in it for the long haul. But interestingly enough what makes this such hard work is also what makes it so attractive to a writer. Web TV is perhaps closer to the theater than to TV as it enables direct contact with the audience. Maybe the instant feedback is, besides the absolute autonomy, the real kick behind producing for the web – and surely also the sense of being a pioneer, as there are no rules and no system in place. In web TV no one tells the writers what to do, at least not yet. At the same time one is taking part in determining the future of a new medium and a new space, and that is surely exciting in itself.

Jane Espenson compares writing for TV and the web in a most interesting way: "The thing I really like about webisodes is that they fit really well with one of my favorite things – taking a minor character and putting them center stage," she says. "In real life, no one is a supporting character – and in a well-written show, the same should be true." So is Web TV ultimately shedding light on characters who had to be ignored in storytelling up till now?

Indeed it seems that the short, closed form of a webisode, which allows for short, closed stories, also allows characters who would normally be treated as minor ones in a TV series to be at the center of attention. Perhaps it also allows for even more detail in storytelling. It is, however, a medium that is still looking for its true form. At the moment it may seem impossible to even imagine its storytelling potential. But didn't it seem impossible to imagine TV's storytelling potential at its beginning?

Like running a marathon

As Robert Carlock puts it, breaking a story or an episode is like breaking a wild horse. Riffing on that metaphor: it may run away if you come too close, but if you have it cornered in a tight space, it may slip away. All in all, it is a delicate and difficult endeavor, and in TV you are making it under the most difficult circumstances.

For one thing, you're constantly working on several episodes at the same time. You also constantly have production looming, while lead time (which is the time between start of writing and start of shooting) is short, and it becomes shorter as you go. You become more and more tired as well. In our conversation, Robert Carlock describes the time schedule of *30 Rock*. They would start writing in June and start shooting in August, at which point they would have had about two and a half months lead time. As the show moved on, however, it would get more and more dicey: now instead of two and a half months ahead they would be about a week and a half ahead. Having such a short lead time is basically a nightmare. What if you cannot make it? What if you fail?

At *30 Rock*, which was shot with a single camera, like a traditional movie, the writers had to produce 22 episodes per season, and they were shooting the show from August till the end of March. When they finished shooting, towards the end of March, the showrunners would take a week off. Then, still having three or four episodes to edit, which would take all of April, they would basically have a break for six weeks and start again in the middle of June. This is not a normal lifestyle, and nobody pretends it is. And yet, like Warren Leight, Robert insists that pressure can be good, and that it can make you see things you wouldn't if you had too much time to think about it.

The distinction between multi-camera and single-camera means a distinction not only in production (for instance, multi-camera will be mostly recorded in front of a live audience), but also in how the show is developed and written. With the multi-camera approach, you shoot the whole thing in a day – and you spend the rest of the week rewriting and rehearsing. And what is funny one day may not feel funny the next day, as Robert points out. So there is pressure, but it is a different kind of pressure.

Robert Carlock reminded me of how the playwright, screenwriter and director David Mamet once said that "doing a movie is like running a marathon, doing a TV show is like running until you die." It is not difficult to see why he might have said that.

Then, one day the show ends and you are out there trying to get new work or pitch a new show. Eric Overmyer talks about how a writer will not pitch at the same time as he is on a show: "You're not allowed to work for anyone else contractually. I guess theoretically I could go pitch something to HBO but they will look at me and say, Aren't you supposed to be working on *Treme*? They would be suspicious that I wasn't kind of keeping my eye on the ball." So when does a TV writer get to prepare new work? In the six weeks he gets to see his family? Obviously, writing for TV is more than a job. It is a lifestyle and a state of mind.

The unwritten rules

Warren Leight is the only writer who referred to "the unwritten rules of American TV" – by which he means certain rules that the showrunners have internalized, and the misrepresentation that this internalization creates. He explains how, for instance, nobody wants to see the crimes of the ghetto, or wives cheating. The excuse is that the audience will not like it, and the control mechanism is the ratings. This is the way the audience can show its discontent.

Still: how true is that? The dictatorship of the audience, which can show its discontent by tuning out or not tuning in at all, is a fear with which every TV writer is familiar. Especially in a time when networks and companies do not give much time for a show to eventually find its audience. Word of mouth has to work right away; if it doesn't, by the time it has started working the show may already be off the air.

That the audience will turn off the TV or stop watching a show if the character of a wife is cheating is difficult to believe. It is of course a fear, but there is no proof – the writers stop writing in that direction before it can be proved. Writers have either created a monster, an audience which goes by the unwritten rules and which only knows one reality, the one that has been served to it for so many years, or they are simply scared of failing. But what about educating an audience, or challenging it?

Warren Leight talks about sameness of content as one of the things which may result from the writers' fear of trying out something that is against the unwritten rules. Sameness of content is also connected to branding. Networks are brands, and people go there to see a certain type of show, just like in the old days when they would expect a certain type of movie from a certain studio. Perhaps this predictability and safety is counteracting the insecurity of today's world; perhaps it is just a way to sell more and better programming – and, ultimately, more and better advertising.

After all, one should not forget that television is a business. And as Terence Winter says, "It's like running any business. They (the network or cable company) are the parent corporation and they have a lot of subsidiary businesses. Those businesses are the TV series. And if you are a subsidiary, if you're turning a profit, if it's well run and everybody seems happy and everything is on schedule, they don't need to supervise you so closely." And when they do not supervise you so closely, that is when the best work gets done. If nothing else, HBO has shown that giving as much creative freedom to the writers as possible (to hell with notes), is ultimately a ticket to success. The success of recent American TV series is the best proof. Might it be time for other media to learn from this example?

After all, writers have their own built-in breaks. Whether they want it or not, they are haunted by the fear of the audience which might not tune in to watch and by so doing kill their show. Terence Winter makes the point that from years and years of watching movies and TV, audiences are, sadly, very familiar with a particular formula and with being spoonfed. It is a never-ending cycle, and it can only be broken by having the courage to experiment – and to fail. When you experiment, there are no guarantees – it has not been done before so you cannot depend on previous experience. But what are the chances you can get another writing job if you fail? That is a decision each writer has to make for themselves. The fact is that the system does not allow for experiments that stray too far from the beaten track. And, ultimately, aren't writers part of the system? Aren't they (also) the ones who sustain it, by not straying too far from the beaten track, for fear it would destroy their careers?

A movie told in chapters

Terence Winter thinks that the best stories leave you wondering what they meant, but he also makes it very clear "that in the very simplest terms, what we do is finding out what the character wants and creating obstacles to him or her getting it" and that "it's a lot of deciding how much information to give out and at what particular time and where it is most effective to introduce that information. 'How much' and 'when' are really the two big questions of telling a story," he concludes.

While most will extol TV writing as the best writing out there, many of the writers I talked with were more cautious and mentioned that even though there's a lot of great TV there's also a lot of bad TV. TV is a writer's medium, but as Paddy Chayefsky said when TV drama was at its very beginning: "The taboos of television, though much is made out of them, are really no worse than those governing the movies or the slick-magazine short story. Only on the Broadway stage or in the novel form is there any freedom of topic, and even the stage has produced little in the last ten years that could not have been done on television."[2]

Even if some of the taboos have remained and although TV is using conventional dramaturgy and filmmaking for the larger part, TV drama has grown up since the days of Chayefsky. For one thing it has discovered its true length and the dramatic unity of the season. Binge viewing (watching one or more seasons in one go) is a result of that development, rather than the reason behind it. Warren Leight speaks about the cinematic structure of the season in *Lights Out*, and how it is built as a three-acter. It is clear that the best TV is actually a movie told in chapters. It is created and should be watched and analyzed as a long cinematic narrative.

Of course, most TV series are multi-protagonist structures and in that sense they cannot be a three-acter in the classic sense of the word. In that context, Jenny Bicks describes the structuring of the overall screenplay/storylines for a season in a most wonderful way, as being like a musical composition: "It's like composing a score, you want to figure out which of your instruments is playing more strongly at what time."

She also talks about the differences between sitcom and drama in relation to the writers' focus. In sitcom you are less worried about structure – and more worried about getting a joke in. It is in drama that your concern is the serialized nature of your characters and the structure of your script.

Of course, time has a different tradition in TV. When you talk acts, TV writers think advertising breaks. In network TV act breaks are still

defined by advertising breaks, and there are usually four acts. *Law &*
Order is a case in point. The teaser is the first one. Then there is an
act on the street. The third and fourth acts are with the DA and in
the courtroom. That comes from when it all started, and it was advertising that created the structure. Today, there is even an additional
break, and the writers need more cliffhangers to end each act before
the commercial.

The fact that cable has no advertising also means that it is less
restricted in terms of dramaturgy and content in general. Jane Espenson
is skeptical: "There are huge opportunities to experiment, but it is still
providing a product to a corporate entity that has certain hopes and
expectations. It's not all that free. But the kinds of products you can
offer them ... that's where it's gotten freer." For instance, "there is more
concern in network that people will not like your character," as Jenny
Bicks points out. "Especially if it's a woman." She talks about the fact
that there still is a desire for network shows to have a beginning,
middle and end, which means that each episode will be wrapped-
up. While in cable shows you do not have to have the character learn
a lesson or come full circle, you're allowed to just be with the character. The writers can have them make huge mistakes and they do not
necessarily have to learn from them. Jenny Bicks is basically describing the main difference between classic structure and the alternative
storytelling structures which have been evolving during the last few
decades. Cable TV has been essential in informing cinematic structure
in that evolution towards less pedagogic storytelling forms – and elements such as nonlinear narrative or multiple protagonists are part of
the game.

It is interesting to see how a different funding system may allow for
greater independence, and for more trust in the creative people and ultimately the audience. "I don't believe they trust the American viewer,"
says Jenny Bicks, referring to network TV. "People know what they like
to watch, but they don't give them enough credit." Giving the audience
enough credit means offering them something they are not used to,
surprising them. Cable TV's success seems to be based on doing exactly
that – and that presupposes the willingness to risk and to give the writers
the opportunity to experiment.

Crossing the borders

It has to be stressed again that the US is not the only place where
good TV gets made – at least not any more. In fact, there is a tendency

at the moment to acquire TV series which have been developed and produced elsewhere and remake them. One source of such series is Israel, and Warren Leight talks about how tricky this may turn out to be for the writers, and about what it means to take a show from one culture and transfer it to another: "I had the luxury of looking at what they did and then…it was almost like having 35 first drafts. And in some cases I discarded them." He explains how some of the storylines wouldn't have worked in the States: for instance, "in Israel there's all kinds of cultural connotations to a woman at 40 who hasn't had a child yet, but that's not the case" in America so you cannot really build a storyline around that. Good writing travels but not all the way.

Tom Fontana, on the other hand, is breaking ground in the sense that he is crossing borders right from the start. With his *Borgia* he is probably the first American writer to run a TV show financed completely by the European market. And he is dealing with European commissioning editors, who are used to working with writers who are much less respected than TV writers are in the US. This is currently slowly changing; however, with a few exceptions (Denmark and the UK being the most well known ones), the European TV writer, although in a better position than his counterpart in the film industry, is still far from having the power and creative freedom of an American TV writer.

What is most interesting in this context is how the Europeans are adopting the writers' room concept. Again, with a few exceptions the showrunner or head writer has usually much less creative freedom than her American counterpart. For instance, it is not unusual for the note-giving, green-lighting studio or network executives (or non-writing producers) to be sitting in the writers' room and brainstorming about story and characters. In America that would be unheard of.

Tom Fontana explains how the European networks are now looking at the American showrunner model, and how they are seeing that maybe giving the writer at least some power is going to give them a better television program. "And that is the Catch-22 of the showrunner deal," according to Tom. "All writers want total creative freedom. But coming with that has to be the financial responsibility of how the show is made. So, you can't be a showrunner and say, 'I don't care what it costs,' because then you're not a showrunner, you're not a writer-producer, you're simply a writer. And if we wanna get European writers empowered, there has to be a change in the attitude of the writer as well. It's not just a change in the attitude of the studio or the network."

The explosion of storytelling

Chayefsky wrote that "television is an endless, almost monstrous drain." And he continues: "How many ideas does a writer have? How many insights can he make? How deep can he probe into himself, how much energy can he activate?"[3] Furthermore, "he (the writer) has no guarantee that his next year will be as fruitful. In fact most writers live in a restrained terror of being unable to think up their next idea. Very few television writers can seriously hope to keep up a high-level output for more than five years." Today's TV requires a level of complexity which is higher than ever before. As Robert Carlock points out, on a TV show you will be doing at least an average of three stories an episode and that is already almost 70 stories a year. With a beginning, middle and end, for a variety of different characters. Who can come up with that all by themselves? The answer seems to be collaborative writing. Ultimately, that is what the writers' room is about. Is collaborative writing the real secret of the medium's success, and what exactly do we mean by it?

A show is heavily serialized storytelling; very few episodes stand alone. In many ways the writers in a writers' room are writing a novel by committee. And although that comparison is often made, Charles Dickens didn't write his episodes by committee. TV writing is very far from the private experience of a novelist, who by himself or herself is pursuing a very private vision. In TV everyone is trying to write the same show, and whether the showrunner will polish or rewrite, whether there is an attempt at a singular "voice" or not, ultimately the evolving system is about many writers working together and functioning as one big brain.

On the other hand, one could argue that 13 episodes would not be too many to be written by one writer, and some cable TV seasons will only have 13 episodes. However, the nature of the medium and the schedule on which it's done ultimately defines it as a medium of collaborative storytelling. It's hard to come up with 13 hours of story in the amount of time one has. Dickens was indeed what we would today call the main content provider for his own magazine. And he would write a chapter every week, which is probably the closest equivalent of what a showrunner tries to do. Only, at the same time there is production and that complicates things. So is the writers' room a necessary evil?

Perhaps not. I was most intrigued by something Janet Leahy said when I asked her how important she considers the concept of the writers' room for American TV's global success. "I think it's everything," she answered. "As far as I can tell, no one person has come up with all the stories for a season of television. That's a fallacy. A writers' room is critical. Not just for the individual stories each writer brings in, but because of the explosion of storytelling that goes on back and forth as the result of bringing these people together."

Story that never ends

The comparison with a novel or with watching a very long movie is also a good one, because serialization means that you cannot watch the episodes in whichever order they reach you. You have to watch the whole season as if you were watching a 12-hour movie. Terence Winter talks about how the effort still goes towards ensuring that each episode may stand alone, as if it were a mini-movie. So when you just happen to watch this one it still has its own beginning, middle and end, and it makes sense. But it's like one chapter in a book. To really appreciate it you have to watch the whole series, as you would read a book.

Actually, it is quite intriguing to think about the effect that long cinematic narrative has on our sense of story. A movie is from its genesis a more closed form. But life is more of a long-running experience, says Terence Winter. Sometimes you meet a person and then they're gone. It doesn't necessarily make sense; from where you are standing you cannot understand it. But not everyone has a big impact on your immediate life. That happens with TV characters too – it doesn't happen that much with characters in the movies.

Ultimately, part of what makes TV so compelling is its very nature as a story that never ends. There are things you can do in TV, given the logic of an ongoing series, which you cannot do in a movie. Most importantly, and that seems to be the key point of long narrative, you can take your characters to so many places that by the time you're done, the audience has a sense of intimacy with them. They have become part of the audience's life. TV gives you that luxury of time which movies, even the longest ones, do not. Perhaps you even reach a point where the audience simply wants to be spending time with the characters, where they and their world feel like home. On the other hand, as an audience member you are making a long-term commitment when you start watching a TV show. Ultimately TV, in its best form, cultivates an addiction. An addiction created by a big brain of collaborative writers telling a story that never ends. An explosion of storytelling, indeed!

Notes

Introduction

1. Nehamas, *Culture, Art and Poetics in Plato's Politeia*, in: ΠΟΙΗΣΗ no. 15 (Summer/Fall 2000): pp. 15–28.
2. "One Vision means that you believe in the author and their vision of the story," says Morten Hesseldahl, DR's cultural director in Gerald Gilbert's 2012 (May, 12) article in The Independent "How Does Danish TV Company DR Keep Churning Out the Hits?"
3. The aim of network TV is to please as many viewers as possible equally; cable TV, because of its different financial model which relies on subscription rather than advertising coin, aims at pleasing relatively few viewers a lot and keeping them as a loyal audience over time. In any case, unlimited viewership in today's new landscape seems like a thing of the past. Reportedly the TV series with the most viewers ever for a single episode was *M*A*S*H* – an impressive 121.6 million viewers watched its final episode *Goodbye, Farewell and Amen* in 1983, surpassing the single-episode ratings record that had been set by the *Dallas* episode that resolved the "Who Shot J.R.?" cliffhanger. In comparison, *The Sopranos* had 11.9 million viewers, while an episode of *Mad Men* has an average of around three million viewers on the domestic market, which is normal for successful American cable series – and which in an interesting way, is comparable to the number of viewers a series like the aforementioned Borgen attracts in its domestic market, which is miniscule compared to the American market (50% of the market there means 2.5 million viewers).
4. "Are Films Bad, or Is TV Just Better?" *The New York Times*, September 8, 2010.
5. In a press conference on the occasion of being honored by the American Academy in Rome with the prestigious McKim award in May 2013.
6. "What Is Cinema?" ("Qu'est-ce que le cinema?") (2004, University of California Press) remains the most influential work of André Bazin, perhaps the best known film critic and theorist of the mid-20th century, co-founder of Cahiers du Cinema, champion of Italian Neo-Realism and mentor to the French New Wave.
7. Eisenstein, "The Dramaturgy of Film Form [The Dialectical Approach to Film Form]," pp. 25–42, in *Leo Braudy & Marshall Cohen: Film Theory and Criticism – Introductory Readings* (1999, Oxford University Press).
8. In fact, the association has already entered industry lingo. For instance, from the Cannes Film Festival 2013 publicity materials of a European production and distribution company, European Star Cinema, which claims to be "developing a full slate of world-class TV programming. Spellbinding

stories enthrall viewers with absorbing drama, cinematic storytelling and world-class movie stars." European Star Cinema calls these novel-like megaseries "Cinema for Television"; the announcement carries the title "High-Quality Series: The New Cinema."

9. Johnson, p. 68.
10. Edgerton & Jones, pp. 67–68.
11. For more information read Matt Locke's online article "After the Spike and After the Like. A Brief History of Attention" https://medium.com/a-brief-history-of-attention/5b78a9f4d1ff
12. Binge viewing is when the audience is watching outside of scheduled broadcasts and watching whole seasons in one go.
13. Alvarez/Simon, p. 25.
14. Thompson, Robert J., *Television's Second Golden Age*, p. 22.
15. Thompson, Kristin, *Storytelling in Film and Television*, p. 12.
16. American TV has always been a writer's medium because of its origins in radio. As Erik Barnouw explains in his book *Tube of Plenty: The Evolution of American Television*, when network television was linked coast to coast in 1951 the US Congress issued more station licenses and allocated more air time and frequencies to the nation's four networks, NBC, CBS, ABC and DuMont, which resulted in a major expansion of the television industry and a rapid increase for new content. As Hollywood felt competitive and dismissive towards the new medium (which explains why they did not deliver the desired movies to fill the program in that early era) and because this era preceded the advent of telefilm and videotape, the live television schedule was a programming vortex with an inexhaustible demand for new shows, 90% of which were broadcast live. That and the identification as a writer's medium were two of the four things that TV drama took from the radio when it started: the other two being that its funding came through advertising and that it was of episodic nature.

Conversations

1. *The Goldbergs* was a comedy-drama broadcast from 1929 to 1946 on American radio. In 1948 it was adapted into a theatre play, *Me and Molly* (and a Broadway musical, *Molly*, in 1973), and it subsequently made it to American TV, where it ran from 1949 to 1956. It was written by writer-actress Gertrude Berg.
2. *The Bowery Boys* were fictional New York City characters who were the subject of feature films released by Monogram Pictures from 1946 through 1958. The series followed a gang hanging out at Louie's Sweet Shop (at 3rd & Canal St.) until an adventure came along.
3. The Comic Strip Live and Catch a Rising Star are among the oldest stand-up comedy showcase clubs in New York City and the world – both notable for their role in starting the careers of many comedians.
4. Howard Korder is one of the main writers of *Boardwalk Empire*. He is also the author of the 1988 coming-of-age play *Boy's Life*, which earned him a Pulitzer Prize for Drama nomination.
5. Greenlit is industry lingo for "approved and financed for production."

Warren Leight

1. *In Treatment* was an American HBO drama produced and developed by Rodrigo Garcia, based on the Israelian TV series created by Hagai Levi. The main character is a psychologist, 50-something Dr. Paul Weston (Gabriel Byrne), and the series shows his weekly sessions with patients, as well as those with his own therapist at the end of the week. The series started airing on January 28, 2008 and ended on December 7, 2010.
2. *Law & Order* is an American police procedural and legal drama television series, created by Dick Wolf and part of the Law & Order franchise. It originally aired on NBC, starting on September 13, 1990, and, in syndication on various cable networks. As of February 13, 2013, 995 original episodes of the *Law & Order* franchise have aired, making it the longest-running crime drama on American primetime television with ongoing characters.
3. *Lights Out* was an American television boxing drama series from the FX network, starring Holt McCallany as Patrick "Lights" Leary, a New Jersey native and former heavyweight champion boxer who is considering a comeback. The series premiered on January 11, 2011. Its final episode aired on April 5 2011.
4. FX (standing for Fox extended) is the name of a number of related pay television channels owned by News Corporation's Fox Entertainment Group. The channel's most popular original shows are *The Shield, Nip/Tuck, Damages Rescue Me, Sons of Anarchy* and *Justified*, as well as the comedies *It's Always Sunny in Philadelphia, Louie, The League, Wilfred, Archer* and *American Horror Story*.
5. *Side Man* premiered in 1998, and was a play about a jazz trumpeter, his alcoholic wife and the son who is parent to them both. The three musicians were played by Frank Wood, Michael Mastro and Joseph Lyle Taylor.

Robert Carlock

1. *The Harvard Lampoon* is probably the world's longest continually published humor magazine. Much of the organization's capital is provided by the licensing of the "Lampoon" name to *National Lampoon*, begun by *Harvard Lampoon* graduates in 1970. *Lampoon* writers helped create *Saturday Night Live*. This was the first in a line of many TV shows that *Lampoon* graduates went on to write for, including *The Simpsons, Futurama, Late Night with David Letterman, Seinfeld, The League, NewsRadio, The Office, 30 Rock, Park and Recreation* and dozens of others. The *Lampoon* has also graduated many noted authors such as George Plimpton, George Santayana and John Updike.

Janet Leahy

1. David E. Kelley has created *Picket Fences, Chicago Hope, Ally McBeal, The Practice, Boston Legal* and *Harry's Law*. He is one of the very few screenwriters to have had a show created by him run on all four of the top commercial US television networks (ABC, CBS, Fox and NBC).

Eric Overmyer

1. David Simon wrote *Homicide: A Year on the Killing Streets*, the novel which was the basis for the NBC series *Homicide: Life on the Street*. He co-wrote *The Corner: A Year in the Life of an Inner-City Neighborhood* with Ed Burns, which he adapted into the HBO mini-series *The Corner*. He is the creator of the HBO television series *The Wire*, and also co-created the HBO series *Treme* with Eric (Overmyer).
2. George Pelecanos is a well known writer of detective fiction set primarily in his home town of Washington, D.C. He worked extensively on both *The Wire* and *Treme*.

Diana Son

1. René Balcer was showrunner for *Law & Order: Criminal Intent* through its fifth season.

Margaret Nagle

1. Holzman is creator of TV's *My So-Called Life* and author of the book to Broadway's *Wicked*.

Susan Miller

1. The International Academy of Web Television was founded in 2008 and is "devoted to the advancement of the arts and sciences of web television production." Membership is by invitation only and members represent a cross-section of roles.

Reflections

1. Emily Nussbaum: *Hannah Barbaric: Girls, Enlightened and the Comedy of Cruelty*. The New Yorker, February 2013, p. 1.
2. Hawes, p. 159.
3. Chayefsky, p. ix.

Bibliography

Allrath, Gaby and Marion Gymnich: *Narrative Strategies in Television Series* (2005, Palgrave Macmillan)

Alvarez, Rafael and David Simon: *The Wire: Truth Be Told* (2010, Grove Press)

Barnouw, Erik: *Tube of Plenty: The Evolution of American Television* (1990, Oxford University Press)

Barreca, Prof. Regina: *A Sitdown With the Sopranos* (2002, Palgrave Macmillan)

Castleman, Harry and Walter J. Podrazik: *Watching TV: Six Decades of American Television*, 2nd edition (The Television Series) (2004, Syracuse University Press)

Chayefsky, Paddy: *The Television Plays* (1955, Simon and Schuster)

Edgerton, Gary R.: *The Columbia History of American Television* (2009, Columbia University Press)

Edgerton, Gary R. and Jeffrey P. Jones: *The Essential HBO Reader* (2008, The University Press of Kentucky)

Edgerton, Gary R. and Brian Rose: *Thinking Outside the Box: A Contemporary Television Genre Reader* (2005, University Press of Kentucky)

Hammond, Michael and Lucy Mazdon: *The Contemporary Television Series* (2007, Edinburgh University Press)

Hawes, William: *Filmed Television Drama 1952–1958* (2001, MacFarland)

Heil, Douglas: *Prime Time Authorship* (2002, Syracuse University Press)

Johnson, Steven: *Everything Bad Is Good for You* (2005, Riverhead)

Kubery, Robert: *Creating Television: Conversations with the People Behind 50 Years of American TV* (2003, Routledge)

Lavery, David: *This Thing of Ours: Investigating the Sopranos* (2002, Columbia University Press)

Longworth, James L.: *TV Creators: Conversations with America's Top Producers of Television Drama* (2002, Syracuse University Press)

Lotz, Amanda D.: *The Television Will Be Revolutionized* (2007, NYU Press)

McBrewster, Agnes F., Frederic P. Miller and Frederic P. Vandome: *Deadline (American TV Series)* (2010, Alphascript Publishing)

McCabe Janet and Kim Akass: *Quality TV: Contemporary American Television and Beyond* (2007, Tauris, London)

Prigge Steven and Ted Danson: *Created by: Inside the Minds of TV's Top Show Creators* (2005, Silman-James Press)

Sepinwall, Alan: *The Revolution Was Televised* (2013, Simon and Schuster)

Thompson, Kristin: *Storytelling in Film and Television* (2003, Harvard University Press)

Thompson, Robert J.: *Television's Second Golden Age: From Hill Street Blues to ER* (1997, Syracuse University Press)